A Pilgrimage in Faith

An Introduction to the Episcopal Church

Franklin C. Ferguson

MOREHOUSE PUBLISHING
Harrisburg, PA / Wilton, CT

Acknowledgements

The quotation from *The Quest of the Historical Jesus* by Albert Schweitzer, © 1957; used by permission of the Macmillian Publishing Co., Inc.

The quotation from *To Speak of God* by Urban T. Holmes © 1974; used by permission of the Seabury Press, Inc.

———————

All biblical quotations have been taken from the Revised Standard Version of the Bible.

———————

ISBN No. 0-8192-1277-6

Library of Congress Catalog Card Number 79-91094
Copyright © 1975, 1979 by Morehouse Publishing

Morehouse Publishing

Editorial Office
78 Danbury Road
Wilton, CT 06897

Corporate Office
P.O. Box 1321
Harrisburg, PA 17105

Printed in the United States of America
by
BSC LITHO
Harrisburg, PA

Table of Contents

To Betsy,

my companion and comfort in things holy and hilarious. Twenty years ago this autumn you came with me to Bell Buckle, Tennessee, just in time to see the leaves turn red on Maple Street and to hear the walnuts ringing on the tin roof of our parsonage, waking us often in the night.

Foreword

I came of age in an Evangelical environment. Clergy representing the Baptist, Methodist, and Presbyterian Churches form a long tradition in my family. My wife's family claims five generations of Methodist clergy. Some years ago we discovered that one of her ancestors who settled in Virginia was a member of the Church of England, but presumably became a Methodist under the influence of that magnificent saint of the saddle, Francis Asbury.

When I was confirmed in the Episcopal Church, I was impressed by the fact that I was asked only one question, "Do you promise to follow Jesus Christ as your Lord and Savior?" This question, from the Order of Confirmation in the 1928 Book of Common Prayer, appears in the 1979 Book of Common Prayer as "Do you renew your commitment to Jesus Christ?" The answer is "I do, and with God's grace I will follow him as my Savior and Lord."

It has been my experience as both a pilgrim and priest in the Episcopal Church that, far from my heritage being denied, it has been deepened and enriched. I have heard this from members of other communions who have entered into the Episcopal Church. Surely the purpose of the Episcopal Church involves more than making Episcopalians out of those who come into it, just as, presumably, it is not the purpose of the Baptist or Roman Catholic Churches to make Baptists and Roman Catholics out of those who enter those communions. Our affiliation with the various expressions of the church represents ways in which we believe we can more effectively come to know Jesus Christ and to make him known, and to receive nurture in the Christian life.

The purpose of this book is to offer a perspective on the Episcopal Church and to serve as a brief introduction and orientation. There has never been and probably never will be any one-volume *summa* of our faith, worship, and history. Certainly mine does not pretend to be. I deeply appreciate the letters I have received from clergy and laity across the country indicating my efforts have helped them prepare for confirmation. They have encouraged this revision of *Pilgrimage in Faith,* first published in 1974.

Confirmation has best been described as a "rite of passage." It does not represent arrival in the faith but, rather, commencement. Our pilgrimage in faith may have begun when, as children, we answered the questions of catechisms. As we mature we find ourselves questioning answers. To follow Christ means opening ourselves to truths which may lie beyond our present understanding and our past experience. Christian faith is rich and replete in the wisdom and testimony of the simple, the saintly, the sinful, and the sophisticated. Their answers might well represent our questions, but their experience provides us with clues to the Kingdom of God.

There is no such thing as my faith or your faith, but rather there is only our faith. Dr. William Pollard, an Episcopal priest and an eminent nuclear physicist, was once an agnostic. One of the reasons he became a Christian was his realization that, just as Abraham ventured out upon the promise of God, all of us live by some kind of faith commitment. Dr. Pollard discovered that, even within the scientific community, hypotheses were often postulated upon what could not readily be proved. Once, when interrogated as to what he believed, he responded by reciting the Nicene Creed because that was reflective of the faith of the church, that which had been given to him. St. Paul wrote to the church in Corinth, "For I received from the Lord what I also delivered to you" (I Corinthians 11:23).

I am indebted to many among the clergy and laity who have both excited and incited me in my growth. Particularly, I am grateful to Kenneth and Jane Duke of my former parish who encouraged me to seek publication of my book. The chapter, "The Church as an Institution," was derived in part from some notes used in a study group at St. Michael's in Cookeville, Tennessee, during the ministry of the Reverend Charles Galbreath. The manner in which I have developed them is my own. I appreciate the help of others, particularly Betty Spencer and Charles Beaumont for their critical observations.

Since the first edition of this book was published, the Episcopal Church, at the General Convention of 1976 voted a canonical change allowing women to be ordained to the priesthood. This decision, along with passage of the Proposed Book of Common Prayer, were the primary causes for the creation of the schismatic Anglican Church in North America (now the Anglican Catholic Church). I do not propose to enter this controversy.

It would seem that the remarkable resilience of the Episcopal Church—its ability, manifested in its history, to hold truths in tension—has been shattered by the events of 1976. Several observations should be made here. First, although our present division is the most serious to date, it is not the first one. In 1688, eight bishops and some four hundred priests of the Church of England refused to take the oath of allegiance to William and Mary because of their conviction that a valid priesthood could only be based upon loyalty to James II and his successors. In the nineteenth century, in America, the Reformed Episcopal Church was created because of the fear on the part of some churchmen that the American church was becoming too "Catholic" in its worship.

A second observation is that the emergence of the Anglican Catholic Church is not simply reflective of our "in-house" quarrels, but is paralleled in other denominations. Increasing agitation for the ordination of women is appearing in the Roman Catholic Church from lay and clerical pressure groups as well as from theological commissions. When we add to this issue those of liturgical change, the vitality of "third-world Christianity," and the Charismatic/Pentecostal movement, our problems and possibilities are no longer parochial or "in-house."

In any age, the church is granted no exemption from the tension between what God has said to the church or seemingly revealed to it—deposited as doctrine—and what God may be saying to us in our own time. Bishops, priests, and laity in our communion and other communions, people of deep commitment and conviction, find themselves divided in conscience over the issues I have mentioned. Some have come to believe that it is their calling to proclaim that the church has departed from the faith, and others to proclaim that the church has finally come to terms with what God requires of it.

Some years ago I heard a priest say, "God does not expect us to be right; he expects us to be faithful." On every side of the issues before us (and issues have always been before us) there are those who proclaim with militant certitude what is "right." But ultimately we walk by faith. Our pilgrimage is "from faith to faith." In our present division within the Episcopal Church the cause of Christ is ill-served by "unchurching" each other or attaching exclusivist claims to our positions. I am fond of a stanza from the prologue of Tennyson's "In Memoriam A.H.H.":

> Our little systems have their day;
> They have their day and cease to be;
> They are but broken lights of thee,
> And Thou, O Lord, art more than they.

To borrow a phrase used by the prophets to describe Israel, we Episcopalians are a "peculiar people." In spite of the apparent contradiction of Catholic and Protestant traditions, we have never exhibited the passion for doctrine that some communions have. While worshiping from a prayer book which is nearly four-fifths Holy Scripture or derived from Scripture, we have refused to hold any one edition of that book as ultimate and binding upon succeeding generations. While believing that the Scriptures contain "all things necessary to salvation," we have refused to make the Bible a "paper pope." While believing, as our Lord taught us, that "you must be born again," we have refused to define the "how" of that birth, realizing that conversion for some might be a gradual revelation, as one beholding the first light of dawn or, as with St. Paul, a blinding revelation. We have refused steadfastly to isolate faith and reason, believing that it is not unreasonable to have faith, nor unfaithful to use our God-given reason.

All of this does not make ours a superior church, but it does mean that we have a vocation to serve as a community of testing what might be the voice of our times or the leading of the Holy Spirit. We are called upon to venture out in risk, in faith that God will correct and reprove us where wrong.

Bishop Stephen Neill once said, "The Church exists for mission as fire exists for burning." Surely ministry, doctrine, the sacraments, and the organization of the church are subservient to the Great Commission of our Lord: "Go therefore and make disciples of all nations, baptizing them in the name of the Father and of the Son and of the Holy Spirit, teaching them to observe all that I have commanded you . . ." (Matthew 28: 19–20).

I. Jesus or Christianity?

The title of this chapter is taken from a book by the same name.[1] Published in 1929, it reflected an assumption on the part of a significant number of church historians and New Testament scholars that Jesus and Christianity represent two separate realities.

The argument, in simple terms, is: Jesus of Nazareth was essentially a prophet and a teacher in the tradition of the Old Testament prophets. Because he denounced the arrogance, elitism, and legalism of the "religious" of his day, he was sentenced to death.

After his death the simple truths of what he taught by precept and parable were eclipsed by the rise of the church—an institution which he had never intended to found. Thus Jesus was soon replaced by Christianity. The man from Nazareth disappeared into the mysticism of St. Paul. The authors of the Gospels, under the influence of pagan cults of the Mediterranean world, turned him into a wonder worker, violating what nineteenth-century man confidently called "the laws of nature."

Thus he who denied divinity was proclaimed divine by those who wanted to justify the institution they had created in his name. He who pointed the way to God was pointed to as "the way" and as "God." The real Jesus lay beneath the ritualism, authoritarianism, and ecclesiasticism which emerged in his name. In the nineteenth century and into the early part of the twentieth century biblical scholarship offered a fresh picture of Palestinian Judaism and the political, economic, and religious background of Jesus' ministry. His teachings were presented as creative assimilations and interpretations of Jewish lore. Scholars affirmed, with those who heard him in the synagogue at Capernaum, that ". . . he taught them as one who had authority, and not as the scribes" (Mark 1:22). We have learned more about the religious cults of his time.

This project to rescue the "historical Jesus" came to a halt with the realization that who he was and what he said was colored by the testi-

1

monies of those who remembered him or those, like St. Paul, who "experienced" him after his death. What this search failed to take into account is the fact that a man is more than the sum of his biographical data. He is not subject to final definition by the times in which he lived. Who we are is in large measure determined by what others believe us to be. As Rosemary Haughton observes, truth "can only be discovered by living, living with other people not just being around them, but really sharing yourself with them." In this way we discover truth "not only *about* but *in* each other."[2]

Marriage, for example, is a way to learn not just about each other, but also what is in the other. Much of the imagery of the New Testament writings, as well as of subsequent devotional writings of the mystics, involves the metaphor of the bride and groom, representative of Christ and his church. Who he is and the truth that is in him become apparent through the experience of a relationship.

There are all kinds of truths about Jesus, represented in attempts to write biographies of him. In one he is a pastoral prophet, a simple peasant. In another he is a mystic and poet along the lines of the prophet of Kahlil Gibran. He has come down to us as an ascetic, advising self-denial in preparation for a better world. He has come to us as one who celebrates the secular, affirming the goodness of the world. He is among us as revolutionary and liberator, as well as one who counsels us to pay proper respect to Caesar and things of the state.

We may picture him in rich marble in our cemeteries. We may imagine him in the twisted agony of a medieval crucifix or arrayed triumphantly in eucharistic vestments, reigning over the altar. He may be pictured with the blue eyes and golden hair of an Anglo-Saxon prince, or with the swarthy, sad, and passive countenance portrayed so powerfully by Rouault.

Actually, the earliest picture of Jesus was discovered in a catacomb. He is depicted as a shepherd, which suggests that the early Christians cared not so much what he looked like as what he did, what he represented in their experience of him. Our biographies of Jesus and our pictures of him tell us more about ourselves than about him.

As for Christianity, its earliest definition is found in the Acts of the Apostles, the earliest history of the church. Here Christianity is called "the way" (Acts 9:2, 19:23). To the first disciples Jesus represented a way or, more precisely, *the* way, for he said of himself, "I am the way, and the truth, and the life" (John 14:6). The early followers of "the way," according to the Acts of the Apostles, were first called "Christians" in Antioch.

Presumably, their name was not of their own choosing, but was given to them because of their firm conviction that Jesus of Nazareth was also Jesus "the Christ," the promised one, the Messiah. He was not only sent by God but, in him, God was to be found. Whatever truths existed *about* Jesus, his faithful followers perceived *in* him the truth about themselves, their "heavenly Father," and the truth of their destiny.

This conviction is dramatically expressed in the first letter of John:

> That which was from the beginning, which we have heard, which we have seen with our eyes, which we have looked upon and touched with our hands, concerning the word of life—the life was made manifest, and we saw it, and testify to it, and proclaim to you the eternal life which was with the Father and was made manifest to us—that which we have seen and heard we proclaim also to you, so that you may have fellowship with us; and our fellowship is with the Father and with his Son Jesus Christ (I John 1:1-3).

Here we can see that the meaning of Jesus, the truth that was in and of him, is not a truth which lies at the end of theological studies or the psychology and sociology of religious phenomena. It is truth discovered in community with those who bear the tradition of proclaiming him.

It has been said that "he who seeks God has already found him." Our efforts to discover Jesus may involve his discovering us. Malcolm Muggeridge, former editor of *Punch* and BBC commentator, describes this in his experience of filming a BBC series in the Holy Land.[3]

One can produce evidence for both sides of the question of whether Jesus intended to found a church. The fact is that a church emerged and, if the mystery and meaning of Jesus Christ is to be known, it must be experienced within what St. John calls "the fellowship."

Albert Schweitzer, in his monumental book, *The Quest of the Historical Jesus,* gave us an incisive survey of the attempts of scholars to locate the "Jesus of history," and to rescue him from the interpretations about him. Schweitzer's conclusion was that there is no hope of finding the historical Jesus in the sense that many hoped he could be found. His book ends with this now classic paragraph:

He comes to us as One unknown, without a name, as of old, by the lakeside, He came to those men who knew Him not. He speaks to us the same word: "Follow thou me!" and sets us to the tasks which He has to fulfill for our time. He commands. And to those who obey Him, whether they be wise or simple, He will reveal Himself in the toils, the conflicts, the sufferings which they shall pass through in His fellowship, and, as an ineffable mystery, they shall learn in their own experience Who He is.[4]

II. The Church as an Institution

The community of those who experience "who he is" constitute the church. While the church is described metaphorically in the Bible, it is an institution.

Institutions and establishments have often come under attack. We hear it said, or perhaps have said ourselves, "I believe in God but not in the church." Recently I heard the reverse of this from a lapsed Roman Catholic who said, in effect, that he believed in the church—in popes, acolytes, incense, and pageantry—but he no longer believed in any reality behind these things. There are those who believe that the institution of the church is at best a distraction and an irrelevance, at worst organized hypocrisy. A recent Gallup poll reveals that, while a high percentage of people believe in God, the majority of those who have dropped out of the church believe that, as an institution, it is unimportant, primarily because of its preoccupation with nonspiritual concerns.

Institutions, however, are a part of the human community. It is inevitable that even protests against institutions eventually become institutionalized! Revolutionary and reform movements which began as earnest expressions of the need for change have ended up as institutions in and of themselves. What is at issue is not so much the existence of institutions but whether some institutions, in our case the church, aren't serving the purpose for which they were created and indeed are even getting in the way of that purpose.

The root meaning of the term *institution* is derived from two Latin words meaning "to cause to stand." An institution is not primarily or necessarily a fullblown establishment. Criticism of "the establishment" often represents a legitimate anger toward an institution which has become ossified, whose vision has been turned inward; it represents energies directed primarily toward its own existence rather than risking exploratory and creative directions.

Jesus "caused to stand" a church. He created a fellowship of those

5

committed to his purposes. Many of the institutional aspects of the church leading toward its manifestation as an establishment developed as that "company of the committed" carried forth its mission. He who caused the church "to stand" created a community that has acculturated itself in varying ways through the centuries. It has, in its better moments, been institutionalized not primarily to protect itself and its investments, but to respond more effectively to the needs of those who seek its help.

Articles and books abound on how the contemporary church should order its life of worship and mission, how it should be structured or restructured, what its priorites should be. "Floating parishes," Charismatic communities, guitar masses, to name but a few, have become for many Christians alternatives to the more traditional forms of church worship. While these movements have indeed brought renewal, some of those deeply involved in them believe that such alternatives (which have proved divisive in some instances) will alone prevent the church from going the way of the dinosaurs.

There is a sense in which today's innovations become tomorrow's traditions. Indeed, today's traditions were yesterday's innovations. Those who argue exclusively for their forms of creative innovation, as well as those who argue the superiority of ancient tradition, should be aware of the consequences of pushing their positions to an extreme. This history of the church manifests its ability in balancing change and tradition. A persistent theme in Scripture is that God wills a church and its survival does not rest exclusively with our efforts either to renew or to keep things the way they once were.

Movements which place themselves outside of the traditional church risk repeating the faults of the institution they criticize. Bereft of the fellowship of the primary body, they can become like the pharisee who gave thanks that he was not like the publican.

Now let us examine the institution of the church more closely. Any institution may be defined in terms of four characteristics:

  (1) a purpose,
  (2) a way into it,
  (3) a characteristic or typical act dramatizing its purpose, and
  (4) a structure of authority and administration.

Purpose

What is the purpose of the church? The cynic might observe, and not without some justification, that its purpose frequently appears to be to promote baptisms (to increase church membership for survival and growth) and to promote bingo and bazaars (to insure solvency). There are those for whom the church represents the religious extension of welfare programs. And then there are those who view it as an instrument of social and political change; thus the once-fashionable statement, "The world writes the agenda for the church." Still others perceive the purpose of the church is to provide an authoritarian father image to those who back away from responsibly solving their own problems.

What, then, is the purpose of the church? Those involved in the community of faith say that the church lives by its imperative to proclaim the good news of what God has done for us in Christ and to provide ways of sharing this glad news and continuing to be nurtured.

Early Christians used the word *church* to describe themselves as a people called out of the world to go back into the world refreshed and nourished by their experience of worship. It was nearly three hundred years after the resurrection when Christians finally had buildings—which came to be called churches—of their own. St. Paul often addressed his letters with the greeting, "to the church which is in your house." In the last decade or so this concept has re-emerged; Holy Communion, prayer and Bible study, and the sharing of our personal journeys in faith have once again been taking place in homes.

Alcoholics Anonymous meets in many Episcopal churches. A visitor notes the honesty, openness, and acceptance which characterize life in this fellowship. The way to sobriety depends not solely upon one's own efforts, but upon one's willingness to be ministered to. There is a real sense in which it is much harder to receive than to give. Our churches are filled with many who are great givers, both in terms of financial and personal resources and abilities, but who find it difficult to receive the ministry of others.

St. Paul spoke of the church as a "body" of which "we are members one of another" (I Corinthians 12:12-26). Jesus used the metaphor of the vine (John 15), which became a familiar motif in the catacombs. The purpose of the church is to proclaim and celebrate the hope by which it lives. Perhaps the most damning indictment of the church came from the philosopher Nietzsche, the son of a clergyman, who said, "The trouble with Christians is that they talk about redemption but they don't look redeemed."

Granted, some of us have trouble with what I call "go-and-glow" Christians who never seem to be depressed, who appear victorious in every situation. But perhaps the ultimate refutation of the atheist or agnostic lies not in our argument, but in the sense of joy and peace which seems to say that we have found Someone, or Someone has found us, and we trust him even in the dark moments, even when he is seemingly silent.

Thus, the purpose of the church is not only to proclaim verbally and visually in song, sermon, and sacrament the reality of renewal, but to manifest a community open to all who seek this new life. The question addressed by the scribes and pharisees to Jesus' disciples—"Why does your master eat with sinners?"—is the scandal by which the church lives. Dr. Ralph Sockman, formerly pastor of Christ Church, Methodist, New York City, was once approached by a man who said that what kept him out of church was its hypocrites. Dr. Sockman's reply was "Come on in, there is always room for one more!" Jesus' calling of the twelve, his presence among priest and prostitute, fisherman and fanatic, tax collector and tentmaker, leper and Levite, indicated the truth of what he said of himself—"I have come not to call the righteous but sinners."

Initiation

All institutions have ways into them, rites of initiation. To return for a moment to Alcoholics Anonymous, the way in is an acknowledgement of the existence of a problem and a confession of the problem.

In the early church those who became members were adults capable of making their own confession of faith. Having done this, they were then baptized and incorporated into the church. The Baptist Church considers this profession of faith to be essential to membership, as do other churches in the tradition of "believers' baptism." Certainly all Christians would affirm the need to experience some kind of ceremony of initiation into the way of Christ. They would affirm the need for a rite to signal acceptance of the affirmation and support of the community. It is important for us to experience the privilege of making a choice, formalizing by our own action what might have been done for us or might not have been done for us.

Of course we *do* make many decisions for our children before they are able to understand the meaning of these decisions. Decisions were made for us prior to our understanding and consent. Long before we understood the meaning of love, we received and experienced it. Long before we understood the meaning of discipline, we responded to it because it was a part of being loved. Then we come to the time of testing. We come to the time of "leave taking," cutting the cord. It might be in the form of rebellion or it might come simply as a quiet questioning of the principles taught us. If overt rebellion on the part of our children disturbs us, then we should be more disturbed by a child's refusal to grow up and discover what it means to make decisions and to live with them.

Baptism

The issue of baptism, its meaning and mode, is complex, the subject of many debates, sermons, and books. Were the biblical evidence conclusive, we would not be divided over this issue; but it is not. Both believers' baptism, with its emphasis upon an adult profession of faith, and infant baptism say some important things about Christian initiation. It is not a question here of who is wrong or right, or who is Scriptural or un-Scriptural, but rather how to maintain both truths— that decisions are made for us responsibly and with love, and that we need to make our own decisions and commitments.

There should be no quarrel with the why of believers' baptism, namely that an act of the will is crucial in making a religious commitment. On the other hand, it is important that we recognize the fact that many of the decisions we make on our own, as adults, might have been influenced by decisions made for us earlier. For example, even within those denominations that practice believers' baptism there is Christian education. The process of education in these denominations certainly involves indoctrination. Thus, when a child comes forward to make a profession of faith, it is a profession shaped by the influence of others.

Indeed, some of these denominations have a ceremony of infant dedication. Although it is not called baptism, it is a way of committing that child to the church and its faith. In a real sense, the child or infant has been the object of a decision made on behalf of that child. In the Episcopal Church, the infant or child is incorporated into the church by a ritual which symbolizes the exodus of the Hebrews from Egypt. It celebrates the truth that infants and children were baptized into a new life of freedom as they passed through the Red Sea.

In later times, Judaism institutionalized its method of initiation by circumcizing males soon after birth. Later in a child's life, around age thirteen, came the rite of *bar mitzvah,* when the boy became "a son of the law." After a period of instruction the Jewish male accepts the meaning of his faith. The Gospel according to St. Luke records this event in the life of Christ. Beyond baptism into the new Israel lies the drama of the Exodus. Harvey Cox, a contemporary theologian, once said, "By the grace of God Christians are honorary Jews."

While adult baptism was the norm in early Christianity, infants soon became subjects. This phenomenon coincided with the emergence of the doctrine of original sin, the belief that the primal sin—the rebellion of Adam—was transmitted at the moment of conception. This doctrine was not unknown in Judaism (Psalm 51:5). St. Augustine spoke of it as a hereditary disease "wherewith infants themselves are infected even in their mother's womb" (Belgic Confession, Art. XV). The prayer for the blessing of water in the baptismal service notes that the water is to be "sanctified" for the purpose of cleansing from sin.

If the Fathers of the church come across to us as seeming overly pessimistic about the power of certain primal drives in human nature, the biblical stories from which they derived their doctrines were stories which are also our stories. We are Adam and Eve. Cain and Abel represent the failure of brotherhood. Every birth represents the potential for wholeness as well as the potential for tragedy. We don't appear, to use Wordsworth's phrase, "trailing clouds of glory" but trailing in our infancy the stuff of tragedy, the potential for violence and murder as well as the potential for love, compassion, and understanding. The psychologically-based human potential movement, now in vogue, often fails to take into account that the message of Jesus is not "fulfill thyself" but "deny thyself," for it is in discipleship to him that our creativity is used for good rather than for evil.

As the process of birth brings us through maternal waters into life, so the rite of baptism represents passage through baptismal waters into a family which affirms that water is thicker than blood. If one meaning of baptism is cleansing, its other meaning is incorporation into the community of faith.

The baptism of infants dramatizes the appropriateness of our making a decision for our children to place them into the covenant, the Way. It is not a question of innocence but of dependency that is essential in understanding baptism and our relationship with our Lord. While it cannot bear the total weight for the justification of infant baptism, the touching description of Jesus' taking children into his arms and blessing them (Mark 10:13ff.) says to us that we are nurtured in faith through dependency, trust, and the openness to mystery which characterizes a child. The presence of godparents indicates that, if we find ourselves in a crisis of faith at some time, unable to believe, others can pray for us, believe for us, in short become for a time our spiritual godparents.

Baptism is not an inoculation against the virus of evil, but inclusion into a Way. It dramatizes and effects Christ's claim upon the potential and promise in each of us in the midst of the claims the world makes about us and upon us. Karl Barth, one of the great theologians of our time, said, "The Christian life is living one's baptism."

Confirmation

Our primary or basic act of incorporation into the church is through baptism. There is, however, another part of initiation into membership in the Body of Christ. It is called confirmation. It is a tradition within the Episcopal Church and in the Roman Catholic, Orthodox, and Lutheran Churches. The Scriptural reference to this act is found in the Acts of the Apostles:

> Now when the apostles at Jerusalem heard that Samaria had received the word of God, they sent to them Peter and John, who came down and prayed for them that they might receive the Holy Spirit; for it had not yet fallen on any of them, but they had only been baptized in the name of the Lord Jesus. Then they laid their hands on them and they received the Holy Spirit (Acts 8:14-17).

This sequence is described again in the nineteenth chapter of Acts; after Paul's baptism certain disciples at Ephesus whom he baptized needed him to lay his hands upon them, after which they spoke in tongues and prophesied. However, in chapter eleven of Acts, we see Peter preaching a sermon during which it is said that "the Holy Spirit fell on them just as on us at the beginning." Thus, in this case, the receiving of the Holy Spirit occurred apart from the laying on the hands of the apostles. One recalls Jesus' saying, "the Spirit blows where it wills. . . ." (John 3:8). We need to be careful in assigning the work of the Holy Spirit to a particular sequence, of making the drama of renewal into a set scheme. Ecclesiastical ritual may invoke the Holy Spirit, but the Spirit is not subject alone to these kinds of invocation.

Early in the third century, in his *Apostolic Tradition,* St. Hippolytus documented the ceremony of Christian initiation prevalent during his time. Certainly it represents earlier procedure.

During the forty-day season of Lent those desiring baptism, or the catechuminate, as this group was called, received instruction by the bishop. On the Thursday before Easter the candidate, if found worthy and ready, was bathed and exorcised—prayers were offered to cast out the influence of Satan. On the Saturday evening before Easter Day the candidate prayed and fasted all night and, at dawn, there were prayers and the blessing of the water. Incidentally, an ancient document called the *Didache,* or "Teaching of the Apostles," dating from around 120 A.D., suggested that a running stream or "living water" be used or, if this was not possible, still water, in which the candidate was either immersed or had water poured upon him.

After the water had been blessed, the candidates were stripped and led into the font or baptistry by the priest. What we now know as the Apostles' Creed was repeated to the candidate and, after each division of the Creed, the candidate was asked if he believed in that particular phrase of the creed. Since the Creed was divided into three parts, he was triply baptized. Emerging from the font, he was given a white robe. The bishop laid hands upon the candidate and prayed for the gifts of the Spirit. The candidate was also anointed with oil of balsam and given a taste of milk and honey to signify entrance into the promised land. The kiss of peace was given and Holy Communion received.

Dr. Massey Shepherd, in his study of the Revelation of St. John, presents references that might have influenced the shape of the primitive initiatory rites. Perhaps the Scriptural references themselves were derived from a familiarity with the then-current practices of Christian initiation. Dr. Shepherd identifies five aspects of the rites: the renunciation of Satan, the profession of faith, the washing, the sealing with the Name, and the investiture with the white robe.[1]

We may note also in I John 2:27 this reference to anointing: "but the anointing which you received from him abides in you. . . ." The word *Christ* means literally "the anointed one." Anointing was an integral part of the ceremony of the investiture of kings. It accompanied the rites of the Catholic and Orthodox Churches.

Basically, the rite of initiation involved two features which have been constant in our tradition and in that of other churches—the water baptism and the laying on of hands. Because, as the church grew, the bishop could not be at every baptism for his role of the laying on of hands, he delegated this responsibility to the presbyter or priest. In the Orthodox Churches, as in the Roman Catholic Church and the Episcopal Church, it is the bishop's prerogative to bless the oil of anointing and, when present, to lay on hands. In the Orthodox Churches, it became customary for the bishop to delegate the anointing and laying on of hands to the priest. The rite of anointing dramatizes episcopal presence—the presence of the chief pastor.

In time, the two elements of initiation—baptism and confirmation—became separated. Increasingly, bishops were not able to make the rounds for confirmation because of the growth of the church and increasing administrative tasks. Many Christians, baptized into the faith of the Roman Catholic Church, were never confirmed; but, in the Eastern Churches, baptism and confirmation were continued as the ministry of the priest. Although many Christians in the Roman

Catholic Church were not confirmed, they still received the Holy Communion; and, in the Orthodox Churches, infants were given communion while in their mother's arms.

In the late Middle Ages confirmation was restored, but this service was not interpreted to mean that the recipient had not previously received the Holy Spirit in baptism and was not already a Christian. The ceremony was intended to convey the strengthening gifts of the Spirit (Galatians 5:22). The candidate was equipped with the spiritual strength to live the reality of the life given in baptism. Baptism was primarily viewed as the negative washing away of sin and confirmation was the positive filling up of virtue.

However, neither the Catholic Church of the Middle Ages nor the Protestant Reformation Churches ever held that confirmation was the primary act or essential component of initiation. A careful reading of the baptismal rites in both the 1928 and 1979 Book of Common Prayer indicates that baptism and the giving of the Spirit are not distinct and separate acts. On page 276 of the 1928 Book of Common Prayer we find, "Give thy Holy Spirit to this *Child* (*this* thy *Servant*) that *he* may be born again. . . ." In our present book we say: "Sustain them, O Lord, in your Holy Spirit. Give them an inquiring and discerning heart; the strength to will and to persevere; a spirit to know and to love you; and the gift of joy and wonder in all your works." (page 305).

In the Offices of Instruction in the 1928 Book of Common Prayer (page 291), the candidate for confirmation is asked, "After you have been confirmed, what great privilege doth our Lord provide for you?" The answer is the privilege of Holy Communion. Generations of Episcopalians have been taught that confirmation was required before communion could be received. This tradition is derived in large measure from a decree promulgated in 1281 by Peckham, Archbishop of Canterbury. The intent of his decree was laudable enough—to educate those receiving the sacrament and to dispel the aura of superstition surrounding it.

His decree did provide for the receiving of communion by the unconfirmed at the point of death, as well as for those who for some reason had been "hindered from the reception of Confirmation." The English Prayer Book of 1662 added the sentence, which also appears in our 1928 book, that those "ready and desirous to be confirmed" could receive communion.

Many of us have never been totally comfortable with the procedure of insisting upon confirmation prior to communion. First, although adults in Inquirers' Classes or adults visiting services are given communion, children who are part of the life of the church are not to receive communion until confirmed. This double standard has not gone unnoticed by our children.

Second, it is stated on page 292 of the 1928 Prayer Book that there are only two sacraments instituted by Christ as "necessary to salvation." This is affirmed in our present Prayer Book (page 858). If we make confirmation an absolute requirement for communion, we would then be making confirmation, in effect, a third sacrament necessary to salvation.

Since the General Convention of 1970, unconfirmed children have been permitted to receive communion after a period of instruction, involving the consent and participation of parents. While, for many Episcopalians, this represents something new in our tradition, it is an ancient practice in the Roman Catholic and Orthodox Churches. While it is doubtful that the Anglican Communion will follow the Orthodox practice of infant confirmation and communion, our church is increasingly affirming the importance of this sacrament in the formative years of a child's life.

Anthropologists speak of "rites of passage." Dramas and rites which celebrate a child's coming of age vary from culture to culture. In the Middle Ages the age for confirmation was established at approximately twelve years. At this age apprenticeship and/or marriage were usually being considered for the near future.

It may be well to do what generations before us have done in formulating a relevant doctrine and practice in regard to this issue. By no means is this to say that our traditional approach (fifth- and sixth-grade confirmation) is wrong. Depending upon the maturity of the child, confirmation may be highly appropriate at this age. However, we should avoid bringing pressure to bear upon our children—pressure from parents, peers, and clergy. Denominations practicing believers' baptism often subtly pressure their children to receive baptism even as early as nine years of age, and certainly many children are influenced by their peers in making this decision.

Regardless of denomination, we share the common problem of a child's readiness requirements. Traditionally, the age of reason for Roman Catholics was seven. But one must also consider age of legality. For many of our young people their rite of passage is the driver's license; the driver's manual becomes, in effect, their catechism! I think it is not inappropriate to question the validity of the pre-puberty push toward confirmation.

There are those in our church who have told me that they wished they had been confirmed later in life. What they mean is that they needed a special rite of affirmation from the church at a particular point in their pilgrimage. In response to this need, the 1979 Book of Common Prayer provides "A Form of Commitment to Christian Service" (page 420). Also, the new service of confirmation provides an opportunity to receive the laying on of hands of the bishop in the sense of reaffirmation of one's baptismal vows.

This does not mean that confirmation as a rite of passage can be repeated. Confirmation dramatizes affirmation of those vows made for us at our baptism. It is an event stating commitment, conveying the strengthening gifts of the Spirit, and, as such, happens only once.

However, just as married couples find their marriage continually refreshed and strengthened by periodic repetition of their vows, and receive grace in that act, so we periodically need to strengthen our relationship to our Lord through the apostolic ministry of his church by renewing the commitment made either by us or for us at baptism and confirmation.

The conclusions to be drawn from the vast and varied history of the rites of Christian initiation are: (1) Baptism is the primary rite of initiation. (2) Baptism and confirmation are not repeatable. Those baptized in other denominations are never rebaptized in ours. (3) Baptism represents the truth that it is by God's action, his mighty acts in history, that we are drawn to him, all apart from our deserving or understanding.

At the heart of conversion or becoming a Christian is a paradox—we can turn to God only because he has turned to us. Jesus said, "You did not choose me, but I chose you..." (John 15:16). At the heart of Christian initiation lies this truth. Our rites of initiation have at their heart the initiating grace of God, choosing us even as we choose him.

The Characteristic Act

All institutions have some kind of corporate act which represents and sets forth as a drama that community's purpose or reason for being. In the Acts of the Apostles it is said that the early Christians "devoted themselves to the apostles' teaching and fellowship, to the breaking of bread and the prayers" (Acts 2:42).

Implicit in this account is reference to three components of worship:

(1) The "devotion" to the teaching of the apostles certainly involved the reading of such Scripture as they had, with commentary. (2) "The breaking of bread" refers to a common meal, similar to our fellowship suppers, but this meal was followed by the Lord's Supper. (3) "The

prayers" here refer to the Lord's Prayer along with intercessions, petitions, and thanksgivings.

When one enters an Episcopal church the first thing that meets the eye is usually the altar. This is not intended merely to be a worship center—a receptacle for flowers and candles. It is the place of a sacred meal occurring every Sunday and at other times during the week. In a real sense, the altar is the reason for the building.

We must remember that the first Christians did not "go to church" in the sense that we use this term today. They *were* the church, the *ekklesia,* gathering in homes or wherever they could meet. These gatherings were focused on the act of eating together. A communal life characterized the early church (Acts 2:44).

After the common meal, the Lord's Supper was celebrated. In time this became an event removed from the common meal. St. Paul describes the reasons for this: Some were able to arrive early for the supper and they ate and drank without seeming to care about their poorer brethren who came late; thus they destroyed the sense of community. He alludes to the fact that some were drunk before the others arrived (I Corinthians 11:17-21).

After he deals with this issue, he provides the earliest reference to the Lord's Supper we have in the New Testament writings:

> For I received from the Lord what I also delivered to you, that the Lord Jesus on the night when he was betrayed took bread, and when he had given thanks, he broke it, and said "This is my body which is for you. Do this in remembrance of me." In the same way also the cup, after supper, saying, "This cup is the new covenant in my blood. . . .For as often as you eat this bread and drink the cup, you proclaim the Lord's death until he comes (I Corinthians 11:23-26).

The celebration of the Lord's Supper was a proclamation of the death of the Lord until he comes again. This act not only dramatized the purpose of Christ's death, but it also represented and effected communion with the risen Lord and, by implication, the deepest kind of communion with those gathered. Thus St. Paul proclaimed that the bread and the cup represented communion in the body and blood of Christ (I Corinthians 10:16).

For nearly three hundred years the Christian community met, often in great peril, to do this. The deep mystery surrounding this meal occasioned suspicion and hostility from the state. Accusations of subversion, cannibalism (because of the language of the rite), and atheism were brought against the first Christians. But the meal was the reason they gathered. An early Christian, prior to being put to death for being present at this meal, exclaimed, "As if a Christian could exist without the Eucharist. . . !"²

Although the Protestant Reformers, and certainly Luther, retained the Lord's Supper as the central act of worship, in time it became less important in Protestantism. One reason for this was the superstition that had emerged around this rite. The Protestant Reformers intended to provide instruction and to lift the rite from what had become too often a rapid and routine exercise on the part of the priest, the congregation for the most part being passive, engaged in private devotions. In one sense, it was really because the Lord's Supper was so important that it came to be celebrated infrequently among Protestants in the latter stages of the Reformation. An emphasis upon the need to educate the laity was crucial, but a less justifiable reason gradually became apparent. Indeed it was not so much a reason as it was an assumption that religious truths were essentially propositions and preachments to be heard and discussed. The emergence of rationalism which followed the Age of Faith and the Reformation, had an influence upon theology and worship. Baptism, for example, became more and more a private act, celebrated apart from the main service, involving only the family and godparents. Holy Communion, while perhaps celebrated at an early service, lost its centrality as the primary act of worship. The usually lengthy sermon became the focal point. The history of the Christian faith indicates that, sometimes for better and often for worse, the worship of the church was influenced by the cultural and intellectual currents of the times.

In our time, across all denominations, there has emerged and is continuing to emerge a deeper appreciation of the centrality of the Lord's Supper. In the 1979 Book of Common Prayer it is noted that "the Holy Eucharist [is] the principal act of Christian worship on the Lord's Day and other major Feasts. . ." (page 13). While the Gospels vary in what they include of the sayings of Jesus, this act (the Eucharist) is found in all of them, as instituted by our Lord. Indeed, not only is the Supper found in all four Gospels, but in the crucial teaching of Jesus beginning with his statement, "I am the bread of life" (John 6:48ff.).

In the Episcopal Church the canons governing a communicant in good standing specify that communion should be received at least three times annually. While many of us believe it should be a weekly obligation, our church has wisely avoided legalism in regard to receiving Holy Communion. There are times when a person might be dealing with some unresolved anger or inner conflict and needs more spiritual preparation or counseling. "Let a man examine himself, and so eat of the bread and drink of the cup", writes St. Paul (I Corinthians 11:28).

Where a priest is available, a celebration of Holy Communion is to be offered on the Lord's Day. Traditionally, most Episcopal churches provide an opportunity to receive at an early service; but, given the increasing participation on the part of children, the Lord's Supper is more and more becoming what it once was—the family service.

On the basis of Scripture and tradition the Lord's Supper has constituted the norm of worship. But why? Certainly our Lord intended what he instituted to be perpetuated. But why did he not choose to provide us with a collection of meditations, with the suggestion that we meditate upon his teachings when we assemble? Why did he choose to identify himself specifically with bread and wine?

One way of understanding this question is to consider how we unite spiritual and material realities. Consider our flag—a bit of bunting. When we see it disgraced most of us are offended, because it represents the principles by which we order our civil life. A wedding ring represents a symbol of what is, we hope, a living union. A birthday cake makes the birthday party; somehow a birthday pie would be inappropriate.

We are surrounded by the symbolic, things akin to sacramental. A sacrament has been defined as "an outward and visible sign of an inward and spiritual grace given unto us. . ." This definition specifically relates to the sacraments given to us by our Lord, but it is true that we experience many things in symbolic ways. We are held together by symbols, by reminders of our history and the things we hope for. While the Lord's Supper is a sacrament, it is more than merely a symbol or reminder because, as we shall see, it does not merely remind us of our Lord but it conveys his presence.

When Archbishop Ramsey said, "Of all religions Christianity is the most material," he was speaking sacramentally. The Incarnation—the act of God's becoming man—is the primary fact of Christian faith. The Spirit became flesh and blood. The parables of Jesus are replete with references to salt, leaven, seed, pearls, and yeast. He did not speak of the Kingdom of God in intangible or theoretical terms but, rather, in everyday language, illustrating its reality by the things of creation. On the night before his crucifixion, he identified his continuing presence with bread and wine—normal components of the supper.

The first miracle recorded in the Gospel of St. John took place at a wedding feast where water was turned into wine. Unlike some of the religious folk of his day who were impressed by the abstinence of John the Baptist, Jesus affirmed the use of wine as a means of creating joy at the feast, affirming by implication the words of the psalmist, "Wine maketh glad the heart of man!" Wine has traditionally afforded a sacramental means of sharing the joy of an event. The cup of the Last Supper dramatized, however, not only the joy of the faith of Israel, the offering up of God's good creation, but it also represented the cup of sharing in the coming suffering of our Lord.

I have used two terms, the Lord's Supper and Holy Communion, to describe the characteristic act; but there are other terms that have been used. The Lord's Supper is derived from the event itself—an evening meal. Although scholars are divided as to whether this supper was indeed the Passover feast or simply another meal, it soon became, in the minds of the faithful, the supper particularly and peculiarly related to the Lord of the church.

Holy Communion, as we have noted, is derived from St. Paul's statement in I Corinthians 10:16, which emphasizes our participation in the body and blood of Christ, our communion in him and thus our communion with each other. Ancient man regarded the act of eating together as an act of intimacy. It implied trust. Although we live in a time of fast foods and TV dinners, we occasionally experience communion in the act of eating and drinking together.

The term Eucharist, a term most often used across the denominational spectrum, comes from the Greek word *eucharistia*, meaning "thanksgiving." A dominant theme of Holy Communion is thanksgiving for, at the heart of the service, is the statement, "on the night in which he was betrayed he took bread. . . .and when he had given thanks. . . ." This is our supreme service of thanksgiving for sharing in God's creation and in his redeeming involvement in creation.

The Mass is usually associated with the Roman Catholic Church. However, in the first Anglican Prayer Book of 1549, Archbishop Cranmer retained it. It disappeared from further revisions. This term is from the Latin *missa*, which means "to send." This term dramatizes the purpose of Holy Communion as that which strengthens us as we return to the tasks of life.

The Orthodox churches often use the term The Holy Mysteries, implying that Christ's presence in the sacrament is a mystery. It lies beyond the boundaries of precise definition. Controversy and debate as to the nature of presence has characterized the history of Christianity. Queen Elizabeth I expressed herself on the subject in this way:

> Christ was the word that spake it,
> He took the bread and brake it;
> And what his words did make it,
> This I believe and take it.

Presence

In this section we will look briefly at some of the ways in which presence has been explained in Protestant and Catholic thought. Although the early church fathers affirmed the real presence of Christ, they gave us no theologies of the presence. It was not until the late Middle Ages and the advent of scholasticism that doctrines emerged in regard to this issue.

It has been said that Roman Catholicism, Orthodoxy, and Anglicanism have maintained belief in the real presence while Protestant Christians have tended toward a symbolic meaning of the Eucharist. In fairness to Protestants, however, none of us believe in the real absence! Presumably, all of us believe in some way in the presence of our Lord; otherwise the symbols of bread and wine would convey nothing. The issue, then, is not over presence, but what one understands presence to mean. The Protestant has often been led to believe that the Catholic is a kind of cannibal. The Catholic has been led to believe that the Protestant engages in a kind of memorial service at which the elements are simply aids for reflection and meditation. Perhaps I have oversimplified these attitudes; but they do represent deep-seated prejudices.

The official doctrine of the Roman Catholic Church since the thirteenth century has been transubstantiation. This doctrine is derived from the philosophy of Aristotle, who was being rediscovered during that period. Aristotle taught that everything in existence has two aspects: substance and accidents. For example, there are all kinds of writing instruments; "accidentally" they may vary—felt tip, ball point, plastic, metal—but they hold in common the substantial truth that they exist as instruments of writing.

As to the issue of Christ's presence, there are various kinds of bread "accidentally" coming to us in forms which vary; but underlying any kind of bread is its "breadness." According to St. Thomas Aquinas, who used Aristotle as a model for his theological system, at the Eucharist the consecrated bread and wine remain bread and wine "accidentally." However, "substantially," beneath the appearance, they have become the body and blood of Christ. Thus, a miracle has taken place. The miracle of the Mass has been effected. (Incidentally, the term *hocus pocus* is a corruption of the words of the priest during the prayer of consecration, *Hoc est corpus meum,* "this is my body.")

Protestant theologians rejected this doctrine because they said that, since the sacrifice of Christ had been made once and for all, transubstantiation implied a fresh sacrifice every time the Eucharist was offered. Article twenty-eight of the Thirty-Nine Articles, drawn up by the Church of England during the reign of Elizabeth I, maintains that transubstantiation "overthroweth the nature of a sacrament and hath given rise to many superstitions." The problem with transubstantiation is that it raises the question of how anything can exist if it has been deprived of its substance. (I might note here that we should remember that St. Thomas Aquinas was accused of being a modernist because of his use of Aristotle's thought.)

Martin Luther countered this explanation with what came to be called consubstantiation. The prefix here means "with" or "along side of." Luther maintained that, while the bread remained bread, it was still a vehicle for the presence. This view has the obvious merit of avoiding some of the problems of transubstantiation, but in the minds of many it seems to imply a divorce of the presence of Christ from the elements that signify the presence.

Other theologians, more radical than Luther, reacting to what they believed to be Catholic tendencies in him, came to speak of the elements as emblems and signs. There emerged a belief, still attractive to many Christians, that what happens at Holy Communion depends upon the faith of the communicant and his or her spiritual state.

This sounds feasible until we begin to consider how difficult it is at times to have faith or to be in a state of faithfulness which could justify our receving communion without hypocrisy. If a valid communion depends upon our spirituality or morality, then the Eucharist can mean bad news for many of us.

The reason we come to communion week after week is that we need to be made whole. Our faith is weak and we need food for the journey. Surely Christ gives himself to us even when we find it difficult to give ourselves to him.

In our tradition as Episcopalians, faith does not have to do primarily with our personal goodness or our faithfulness in terms of its perfection. Our Lord accepted the man who said, "I believe, help thou my unbelief." Faith has to do with our dependency, our willingness to be led by our Lord. The invitation in the liturgy is to all "who intend to lead a new life." The child holding out his hands and the laborer with his calloused hands both represent dependency, the desire to receive.

We believe that Christ's presence is not created by our faith or by the might of our imagination. Christ is present because of his promise. He is as good as his word. When we celebrate the Eucharist in memory of our Lord, what is involved is not a memorial service for a martyr; if it were we could place a picture of how we think he looked, or perhaps some other symbols of his life, upon the altar, meditate upon them and leave. It is crucial to understand that the word *memorial* in the Eucharist comes from the Greek word *anamnesis,* which means "to recall." At this service our Lord is recalled. He becomes our contemporary and our communion with him is as real as it was for those in that upper room two thousand years ago.

Thus the Eucharist, as the characteristic act of the church, is fraught with mystery, even as is baptism. We experience in a sacrament a multiplicity of meaning. Dr. Urban Holmes, III, in his book *To Speak of God,* writes:

> The nature of a symbol is a slippery thing for many of us. Symbols are the most important part of meaning to us all, because they lie at the heart of reality—they are the most "real" thing we know!. . .A symbol has many references, explicit and implicit, which make it possess ambiguity. It engages us first at the level of feeling, and these feelings are often varied and perhaps conflicting. A symbol is an analogy or metaphor, stimulating our intuition and imagination. A symbol is not something to make, it is something we discover.[3]

In every age the church rediscovers the richness of the symbols which constitute and dramatize its purpose. In every age our scientific endeavors yield more understanding of the nature of our universe. But, today, at the heart of that enterprise lies the mystery of creation and the realization that much that seemingly had been neatly defined and understood in the past now possesses a complexity transcending precise explanation. The mysteries of baptism and the Eucharist are grounded in God's purpose for us, and they will never totally yield to our definitions and doctrines of them.

Administration

Every institution has a structure of authority, a hierarchy, a way of administering its purposes. Institutions have simple beginnings, evolving out of a purpose, and require, in time, ways of dealing with authority and maintaining discipline. As we said earlier, movements inevitably become institutionalized, become organized.

The Gospels do not reveal a concern with organization on the part of Jesus. Seemingly, his twelve apostles were a random selection. His treasurer betrayed him and fled with the funds. Peter, who appeared as preeminent among the twelve, denied him. Unlike those who created the Qumran Community near the Dead Sea, a community dedicated to preserving the faith of Judaism in its orthodox form, Jesus showed little concern with creating a disciplined and organized community.

The early Christians believed that his Second Coming was imminent. His resurrection was a sign, a foretaste of the new order. In his encounter with the forces of Satan, manifested in the presence of illness, he dramatized his own proclamation that "the kingdom of God has come among you." The early chapters of the Acts of the Apostles, centering on the preaching of Peter and his healing ministry, indicate the reality of the presence of the risen Lord, confirming the assurance on the part of the disciples that the powers of this world would soon be dethroned. The first Christians were motivated by the imperative to proclaim that God's promised kingdom had been inaugurated in Jesus and that he had empowered them by his Spirit to "go therefore and make disciples of all nations, baptizing them in the name of the Father and of the Son and of the Holy Spirit" (Matthew 28:19).

Our primary information about the organizational structure of the early church is found in the letters of St. Paul. They give us glimpses into the problems he faced; indeed, we would have few letters from his hand had there not been conflict and controversy in those first congregations.

His most important insight into what should be the nature of the Christian community is revealed in the first chapter of his first letter to the church in Corinth. The model here is an organic one. He notes, "Now there are varieties of gifts, but the same Spirit; and there are varieties of service, but the same Lord" (I Corinthians 12:4-5). In this body there is no place for the assumption that one member or function of that member is more important than the others. He concludes that the offices of evangelism, healing, speaking in tongues, prophecy, and other aspects of ministry and administration are integral to the body.

Ministry

As Christianity rapidly expanded, and as it became increasingly apparent that the Lord's return was not imminent, the need for organization became crucial. Obviously, the apostles exercised pastoral care of the churches, which in many instances were splinter groups of the synagogues, comprising both Gentile and Jewish Christians. Thus, it was natural that the government of the churches came to resemble that of the synagogue. Overseers presided at the Eucharist; there were boards of presbyters (from which we get the word *elder*), and deacons (a term meaning "servant"). This latter office is described in the sixth chapter of the Acts of the Apostles, where the twelve insisted that seven men be set apart to deal with administration of charities in the church.

Bishops, or *episkopoi*, from which we get the word *episcopal*, and deacons are discussed in detail in regard to what should be their character and behavior in the letters of St. Paul to Timothy and Titus. There are three kinds of ministry—bishops, presbyters, and deacons—mentioned in these letters.

The New Testament writings give us no clear picture of how the early churches were organized. Today's Christian church is governed by three different administrative forms: episcopal, presbyterian, and congregational. While each of these words also signifies three particular denominations, they basically refer to three modes of government.

Let us begin with the first category—episcopal. As we have noted, this work is a transliteration of the Greek, *episkopos,* meaning "overseer." The word *bishop* is from the Middle English word *bischop* or *biscop.* Episcopal churches are those communions in which the office of bishop is of primary importance.

The second category, presbyterian, derives from the New Testament Greek word *presbyteros,* meaning "elder." Elders comprise the government of the Jewish synagogue. While they might elect a spokesman, essential supervision and policy were in their hands as in those of a corporation.

The third category, congregational, refers to the congregation as an independent reality. At the time of the Protestant Reformation, a concept of self-government emerged on the part of splinter churches. It was believed, on the basis of New Testament writings, that the early church was essentially congregational in nature, not subject to outside directives. The Baptist Churches and the Congregational Churches are among those representative of this category.

The question, then, is what do Presbyterian and Congregational Churches do about bishops? How do they explain them or explain them away? Their answer is that they have what the New Testament really means by bishops—they see the authority of the bishop residing in the congregation itself. Their argument is that, after the death of the twelve apostles, there was no apostolic succession; but their authority came to be represented by the corporate reality of presbyters or elders. While Congregationalists recognize that men like St. Paul assumed pastoral supervision of the early churches after the death of the apostles, the office of bishop became localized in the presbyters, elected by the congregation.

The episcopal family of churches—the Anglican Communion, the

Orthodox Churches, and the Roman Catholic Church—believe that the original twelve apostles appointed others to continue their ministry. Apostolic succession, crucial to the life of these communions, refers to the conviction that the divinely decreed ministry of the apostles is continued today in the office and order of bishops, which represents an unbroken line of succession.

Those who disagree in this belief ask how it can be proved. St. Paul might have appointed and ordained Timothy to be his representative, but can it be shown that those who followed in this succession actually appointed and ordained others with a similar intent? To be sure, there are instances of churches in the early era—for example, the church in Alexandria—where elders or presbyters elected their bishop from their own ranks. No bishop was called upon from the outside to validate their decision.

The Methodist Church has bishops but understands them in this way. While denying apostolic succession in the sense that that tradition is understood by churches in the Catholic tradition, Methodism has a strong concept and practice of episcopacy. John Wesley, given the immediate need to organize Methodism in America, laid hands on Francis Asbury, admitting that his act was inconsistent with the policy of the Church of England. He used the church in Alexandria as a precedent for his action.

It must be noted that there is a kind of arrogance traditionally manifest among Anglicans and others who uphold apostolic succession, dogmatically asserting that apostolic succession is absolutely necessary for the existence of any church. There is a sense in which apostolic succession has been presented as a kind of "chain-gang" doctrine, which in its own way is as weak as the absolute claim on the part of some congregationalists that their organization represents the true tradition of the early church.

If the Scriptures conformed to a precise model on this issue, we would all be united. How then do Episcopalians understand and justify the practice and concept of episcopacy and apostolic succession since this issue has presented a problem in considering reunion with other churches?

Our approach involves the observation that the structure of bishops, presbyters, and deacons is not inconsistent with the overall picture of the church set forth in the writings of the New Testament. It is evident that St. Paul and other apostles exercised authority, appointing and ordaining representatives in their stead, who in turn needed others to help them. The Episcopal Church views this threefold structure of ministry as germinal in the New Testament church.

A problem which confronts any attempt to discuss the New Testament church is the precise meaning of that term. At what period did the New Testament church come to an end? The Scriptures making up the New Testament writings were not formally authorized as such until the middle of the fourth century, at which time the threefold model was normative in all churches. In the early part of the second century, correspondence of early bishops such as Polycarp, Ignatius, and Irenaeus reflected the administrative and ministerial nature of the church.

In 179 A.D., Irenaeus, bishop of Lyons, claimed, "We can enumerate those, who by the Apostles were appointed Bishops in the churches and their successors even to our own time." He was a disciple of Polycarp, bishop of Smyrna, who was reputed to be a pupil of St. John. St. Ignatius, bishop of Rome, martyred in 110 A.D., in his letters to the churches of Asia Minor, notes the establishment of what we have come to call monarchial episcopacy.

By 180 A.D., according to the testimony of these early Fathers, there had appeared in Syria and Asia a monarchial episcopate, a system which had a major bishop overseeing numerous congregations. For a while each congregation had its own bishop, who was celebrant at the Eucharist and who administered baptism and taught. In time, this authority came to be shared with presbyters and deacons, who disbursed charities, and bishops of the major congregations in important cities assumed authority over other bishops in their jurisdiction.

Because of the growth of the church, many congregations were left without bishops. Thus the presbyter, ordained by the bishop, with the assistance of other presbyters in the area, represented the episcopal presence in the congregation. The congregation could elect and appoint suitable presbyters, but it was the bishop's privilege to examine and ordain the candidate.

In the Anglican, Roman Catholic, and Orthodox Churches, the presbyter represents the bishop. He is an extension of the apostolic presence of the chief pastor. He does not belong to the congregation.

Although, in the Episcopal Church, the bishop need not be present to administer baptism or celebrate the Eucharist, it is his ancient privilege to do so upon his visitation. While in our tradition the bishop confirms those coming into this branch of the church, in the Orthodox Churches the presbyter confirms. The oils of confirmation, however, have been blessed by the bishop, thus effectively symbolizing his presence at the rite.

Historically, the Anglican Communion has interpreted apostolic succession in three ways: (1) for the well being of the church (*bene esse*); (2) for the being of the church (*esse*); and (3) for the fullness of the church (*plene esse*).

The first of these holds that episcopacy is a workable and reasonably efficient way of administration. The second of these states that bishops are of the essence of the church—"no bishop, no church." Where churches exist without bishops they exist only by the "uncovenanted" grace of God. The third view, representing my personal understanding, sees episcopacy as that mark of the church which represents her fullness.

A friend of mine in another ministry once said, "You may have the apostolic succession but we seem to be having the apostolic success!" This is a necessary reminder that no one model of ministry has a monopoly on God's purposes in history. Our Lord said of the religious leaders of his day, who trusted in their tradition, that God could raise up sons of Abraham out of stones if he chose to (Matthew 3:9). All forms of ministry have their limitations and can get in the way of the mission of the church.

Having said this, I am committed to the concept and practice of episcopacy, not only because I believe it to be seminal in the order of the primitive church, but because I believe in the transmission of apostolic presence which dramatizes the continuity of the church. Its hazards seem to me to be less than those of congregationalism, which often gives too much power to its pastors, or else dismisses them too easily.

A majority of the Christian church is episcopal in nature, but this does not make that part of the church any more Christian than another part. It does mean that apostolic succession and the historic episcopate cannot be discarded to effect unity with those who disagree with us. As with the doctrine of Christ's presence in the Eucharist, we recognize there is more than one way to express this historical reality.

In 1888, a worldwide conference of bishops of the Anglican Communion meeting at Lambeth Palace declared that there were four essentials in realizing union or full communion with other churches: the Holy Scriptures as a standard of faith, the Apostles' and Nicene Creeds as expressive of the revelation disclosed in Scripture, the sacraments of baptism and Holy Communion, and the historic episcopate.

Before I conclude this chapter on the four marks of an institution, it is necessary to briefly discuss priesthood and the government of our church.

Priesthood

My diocesan newspaper reported some time ago that there are 28,614 ministers and 88 priests in the Diocese of Atlanta. In one sense this information announces that, in this particular diocese, there are 28,702 priests, if by that word we are closely adhering to its Scriptural sense in I Peter 2:9, that all baptized persons represent "a royal priesthood." This diocesan information, however, is intended to designate that all baptized and confirmed persons are ministers but that some of them represent a particular ministry called priesthood.

Protestants have taken strong exception to the term *priest* as applying to clergy. Catholics have priests and Protestants have ministers. Many outsiders who consider the Episcopal Church and the Anglican Communion to be Protestant are confused by the discovery of a priesthood in that church. The Episcopal Church understands itself as an expression of the Catholic and Orthodox faiths in its understanding of the creeds, the sacraments of initiation, the Eucharist, and its approach to Scripture.

While we shall note in due course those aspects of the Roman Catholic Church with which we differ in interpretation, our basic understanding of our church and ministry lies in our practice of the faith and order of the whole church before the fragmentation caused by the Protestant Reformation.

To many, the word priest conjures up all sorts of unpleasant images. It implies priestcraft, the exercise of mysterious and absolute powers by a person whose humanity is considered different from ours. Up until now I have used the term *presbyter* or *elder* to describe the order of priest. The term *priest* is derived from a contraction of presbyter. A presbyter and a priest in our tradition are the same.

The reason the specific term priest is important to us is that it designates the primary role in ministry of the Episcopal presbyter, that of celebrant in the Eucharist. The Eucharist dramatizes or re-presents the sacrifice of Christ. In Old Testament worship, the priest had a definite and essential role as the one who offered up the sacrifice. At the center of Christian worship is the sacrifice and resurrection of Christ.

The Old Testament describes the institution of a priesthood for the purpose of presenting sacrifice on behalf of the people. This duty was eventually given to the tribe of Levi. In the New Testament, the Epistle to the Hebrews provides the background and rationale for the Christian priesthood. Here it is emphasized that Jesus ended the Hebrew system of sacrifice by offering himself at Calvary as priest and victim. Because Christian worship centers in the re-presentation of Christ's sacrifice, by logical implication the president or celebrant of the rite, either the bishop or priest, performs a priestly office. Although the sacrifice of Christ is unrepeatable, St. Paul says that it is to be "shown forth" until our Lord comes again.

In the Middle Ages, the priesthood became invested with extreme powers, closely representing those of the shaman, a magician, in some cultures. The priest came to have a craft. He alone could offer the Holy Sacrifice, which occasioned fear and obedience. We needed Luther's rediscovery of the Scriptural truth that all of us, by virtue of baptism, share in the priesthood of Christ. At baptism we are proclaiming that the candidate shares in "the eternal priesthood of Christ."

All ministry is grounded in our common baptismal priesthood in Christ. In the Episcopal Church, a priest may not celebrate and receive Holy Communion alone, there must be at least one communicant present. The priest is not there as his or her own agent, but is there representing the priesthood of Christ in all Christians.

Our priesthood is mysteriously bound up with the priesthood of all believers. While the order of the priesthood of the clergy has been abused, contradicting the evangel or the good news that is the gospel, it must be observed that, regardless of the denomination, whether the clergy be called priest, pastor, preacher, or minister, the clergy have too often assumed a role and attitude inconsistent with the image of the good shepherd.

There are examples of this in political and community issues where clergy have assumed dictatorial powers or, on the other hand, where they may have represented a kind of professional piety which removed them from the trust of their people. All of the bad things of priestcraft can and do appear among Protestants in preachercraft.

My purpose as an ordained priest is to help those under my care to discover their priesthood and ministry, to enable them to discover and affirm that, in Christ, they have a ministry, a service. A small example: I do not like to say a blessing at the table in a home other than my own because the head of that household, whether male or female, is its priest. The principles and practice of sacrifice, mediation, reconciliation—priestly acts—are represented in the lives and ministries of the laity.

My ordination is to re-present the priesthood of Christ as celebrant of the Holy Mysteries, as well as upon other sacramental occasions. I also represent the priesthood of my people in that, as I offer and consecrate the bread and wine at the Eucharist, holding up their offerings of alms and pledges, the parishioners are gathered up and presented in that act. I dramatize by my ordained role the truth of priesthood, that all of us are called upon to be ministers of reconciliation and faithful stewards of what God has given us—a ministry extending beyond the rites of Sunday.

The ordination of women to the priesthood has, as I mentioned earlier, occasioned formal schism. Although support for such ordination seems to be growing in the Roman Catholic Church, our decision to go ahead has been disapproved of by Episcopalians who wished that we could have done this in concert with other Catholic bodies. At present, not all churches of the Anglican Communion have followed suit, most notably the Church of England. However, in 1976, the Episcopal Church, by voting to permit the ordination of women to the priesthood, illustrated the Anglican tradition that national churches within the Anglican Communion need not act in total agreement with other churches.

There are those who believe that the ordination of women to the priesthood is an impossibility even if it were sanctioned by other Catholic bodies. The redoubtable priest and theologian, Dr. Claude B. Moss, whose book, *The Christian Faith,* is a classic in Anglican doctrine, wrote in 1943, "Women cannot be admitted to Holy Orders. No part of the Church in any age has ever opened Holy Orders for women."[4] We might note that, in 1970, the diaconate, the first order of ministry, was opened to women in the Episcopal Church.

The argument for a male priesthood claims the obvious: Jesus of Nazareth was male. Although the priesthood of Jesus fulfilled and brought to an end the priesthood of the old Israel, priesthood in the Judeo-Christian faith has never included women. Those who oppose a female priesthood note Jesus, while manifesting a ministry to women, scandalizing the religious of his day by talking with women openly, even allowing them to touch him, did not appoint a woman to serve as an apostle.

Unfortunately, the issue of women's liberation, with its legitimate concerns, has clouded the issue of ordination. Secular and civil rights language about "human rights" often obscures the truth that ministry is primarily a calling—whether one is male or female. Thus, while Jesus denied the structure or prejudice in his time, affirming the dispossessed, the outcast, affirming the image of God in all people, he did not call a woman to be part of the apostolic company.

Those opposed to the ordination of women to the priesthood, while readily affirming the administrative role of women in the history of the church (women abbots had more power in places than bishops), and while affirming the spiritual heritage given to the church by women, nevertheless insist that a priest must be the icon or image of Christ, who was male.

Those for the inclusion of women in the priesthood offer the observation that Mary Magdalene was the first to announce to the disciples, "I have seen the Lord. . ." (John 20:18). The primary criterion of an apostle throughout the New Testament is that he must have witnessed the risen Lord. If Jesus did not include women in the company of the twelve, neither did he issue any teaching which would exclude them in the future. It is contended that both Jesus and St. Paul were creatures of their culture and they knew the divisive effects of such a decision. It must be noted that, in other cultures, women priests presided over mystery cults with highly exotic rituals.

At the heart of the arguments advanced for the inclusion of women lie theological understanding of baptism and the meaning of the Incarnation. With regard to baptism, St. Paul wrote: "For as many of you as were baptized into Christ have put on Christ. There is neither Jew nor Greek, there is neither slave nor free, there is neither male nor female; for you are all one in Christ Jesus" (Galatians 3:27-28).

If our primary priesthood is derived from baptism in Christ and all who are baptized are "a holy priesthood, to offer spiritual sacrifices. . ." (I Peter 2:5), then it would seem to follow that women should not be prohibited from representing the order of priesthood in the church. Baptism neutralizes (or should neutralize) the prejudices of culture.

With regard to the doctrine of the Incarnation, what is fundamental is that, in Jesus Christ, God took our nature upon him. This is the primary truth. His maleness is of secondary significance. When we say in the Nicene Creed ". . .and became man," we are saying that God became human.

To be fully human is to recognize the truth that, in every person, there are male and female attributes. Carl Jung, in his concepts of the *anima* and the *animus,* deals extensively with this truth. The *animus* represents the principles of initiative, rationality, and aggressiveness—traits often associated with maleness. The *anima* represents creativity, imagination, passivity, and receptivity—feminine traits. To be fully human, whether we are sexually male or female, is to affirm this completeness.

Our Lord, as the perfect human, dramatized this truth. When he looked down upon Jerusalem before his crucifixion, he used the image of a hen gathering together her brood. One of the names of God in the Old Testament is *Elohim,* a plural form, encompassing the attributes of male and female. The mystics of the church consistently manifest an awareness of the female nature of God (who, though at least male/female, is Spirit and beyond sexuality).

This issue has not been resolved by the appeal to Scripture. Proof texts can be adduced on both sides. The Episcopal Church has affirmed that it is an idea "whose time has come."

The issue of the ordination of women to the priesthood is important not just for that issue alone, but as an illustration of the truth that a living church will always be confronted by issues requiring it to engage in the continuing meaning of tradition and Scripture—particularly Scripture, because this is the earliest tradition and its witness is primary.

In the Acts of the Apostles, Gamaliel, a teacher of the Law, was asked by Jewish authorities to assist in the persecution of some Christians. His response was that, if what the Christians represented was of God, "you will not be able to overthrow them," but if it was of themselves, it would fail (Acts 5:33-39).

This is a good way to test the validity of any ideal whose time has come. The genius of Anglicanism lies in its comprehension of diverse convictions, testing their truth or untruth in the life of the church, in the working out of history. This issue, like others to come, may be of the spirit of the times or of the Holy Spirit. We trust it is of the latter.

Isaiah may well be speaking to us when he says, after God's revelation to him, "Remember not the former things, nor consider the things of old. Behold I am doing a new thing; now it springs forth, do you not perceive it?" (Isaiah 43:18-19).

Tradition is important, but the prophets remind us of the danger of falling into its trap.

Government

Although we have been introduced to the ministerial or clerical "order" of the Episcopal Chruch, we have not yet looked at what constitutes its visible, working operations. Although denominations differ in the ways they understand hierarchy, or lines of accountability, even the most informal kind of organization has a way of governing itself, of organizing itself for its mission. Even those churches which claim to be autonomous and independent from each other have "brotherhoods," "conferences," or "conventions."

I have frequently used the term the *Anglican Communion*. This refers to the worldwide family of Anglican Christians, now numbering some 60 million members in 360 dioceses around the world.

Although the member churches vary in their cultural makeup, and although the contents of their Prayer Books may differ in minor detail (and of course appear in many different languages), there is a common faith and heritage binding us together, symbolized by the archbishop of Canterbury. It is important to note that the archbishop of Canterbury, unlike the pope, has no authority to speak with infallibility or to make unilaterial pronouncements binding upon member churches. Like the presiding bishop in the American Episcopal Church, the archbishop of Canterbury, while Primate of the Church of England, represents a kind of "first among equals" in relation to other bishops throughout the Anglican Communion.

Traditionally, every ten years all of the bishops of the Anglican Communion are invited to meet at a Lambeth Conference, named after Lambeth Palace, the London residence of the archbishop of Canterbury. There, bishops from all over the world explore issues confronting the church and endeavor to work toward a common mind. The statements of these conferences are not binding; they are not statements of doctrine. But they represent, in many ways, the mind of the church as expressed through the episcopate.

Our system of government is characterized by checks and balances between clergy and laity, reflective in many ways of the Constitution of the United States, which was in large measure the work of Episcopalians like Washington, Hamilton, and Madison.

Every three years, the Episcopal Church meets in General Convention—a convention consistsing of clergy (bishops and priests) and lay delegates from every diocese. The General Convention consists of a House of Bishops and a House of Deputies (the latter composed of clergy and laity). Legislation involving proposed changes of the Constitution and Prayer Book must have majority concurrence in both houses. Changes in the Constitution and Prayer Book cannot become effective until they have passed two successive conventions, meanwhile having been referred to the dioceses of the church. The presiding bishop presides over the House of Bishops. Between conventions, the continuing work of the General Convention is carried out by the Executive Council, composed of bishops, priests, and laity.

The diocese is a geographical unit, encompassing parish and mission churches. In some cases a diocese might cover an entire state; in others it might be composed of leading metropolitan areas. Each diocese is presided over by a bishop. He may have (by will of the diocesan convention) a coadjutor bishop, a bishop who automatically succeeds the bishop upon his death or retirement. Or there may be a suffragan bishop, who is elected by the diocesan convention to serve as an assistant to the bishop but who does not automatically succeed the bishop. The diocese convenes annually, with representatives elected by the missions and parishes of the diocese. Clergy are automatically delegates.

Because bishops are governing officials in our church, and because we are called the Episcopal Church, it often comes as a surprise to Episcopal converts how little power our bishops have, in comparison to those of other churches. While our system is hierarchical, it does not empower bishops to act with unilaterial authority. The authors of the constitution of our church provided a system whereby the church could not be ruled by laity or clergy. For example, no bishop can be elected without the vote of two-thirds of the clergy and two-thirds of the lay delegates at diocesan conventions.

Traditionally, there are two kinds of churches in a diocese—parish and mission churches. A parish is self-supporting (or, possibly, aided by the diocese). The priest in charge of a parish church is called a rector. The priest in charge of a mission church is called a vicar or priest-in-charge. The vestry (named after a room where vestments were kept in medieval English churches) is the governing body of a parish and is elected by the parish at its annual meeting. In mission churches the vestry is called a mission council.

The bishop may assist a vestry in its search for a rector. Usually, in mission churches, the bishop assigns a priest. When the vestry issues a call to a candidate, that call must be issued with the bishop's knowledge and consent. Some dioceses have vacancy consultation services which are offered to the parish through the establishing of a profile of that parish to present to potential candidates. The vestry authorizes the creation of a search committee which issues the call.

Unlike clergy in some other denominations, the priest in a parish cannot be fired. His basic stipend cannot be altered as a punitive measure. Our system, involving as it does episcopal assistance, can provide the means of a graceful exit.

Bishops in our church are not primarily administrative figures, although administration is important. A bishop is primarily a pastor, called "Father in God." The purpose of a bishop is to provide counsel both to clergy and laity. Increasingly, dioceses are employing administrators to free the bishops for more pastoral ministries.

A traditional expectation of a bishop is that he be "defender of the faith," a phrase which implies a conservative posture in regard to doctrine and discipline. While this has characterized the episcopate of many bishops, it must be noted that, within Anglicanism, bishops have also manifested what could be called "theological adventurism," often taking liberal positions in regard to social and political issues. A bishop speaks both to and for the church. For example, while English bishops presently have a majority in favor of the ordination of women to the priesthood, clergy and laity have not concurred.

St. Paul wrote to the church at Corinth, "For I became your father in Christ through the gospel" (I Corinthians 4:15). The term *father* is frequently used as a form of address of the clergy in our church as is the term *mister*. On the basis of Matthew 23:8-9 ("call no man your father on earth"), Protestants have not been comfortable with addressing their clergy as "Father." However, in this passage from Matthew Jesus says, "Neither be called masters. . . ." *Mister* is a derivation of *master*. Surely what our Lord is saying is that the titles we give to each other should carry no ultimate authority or usurp the truth that we have one heavenly Father and Master of us all.

Much more could be said about some of the ways that mutual ministries of clergy and laity are manifesting themselves in parish and diocesan life today. In an address to the clergy of the Diocese of Atlanta on February 28, 1977, Bishop Bennett Sims described the renewal of the church, both past and present, as in significant measure the ministry of the laity.

> The monastic movement was largely lay led. St. Francis had to be persuaded to be ordained deacon and steadfastly refused the priesthood. Luther was a monk who was laicized—and married a laicized nun. Calvin was a lawyer, George Fox a cobbler. The Wesleyan movement [Methodist] left the Church of England because we could not bring ourselves to ordain the untrained laity whom Wesley had raised up in such unprecedented numbers by conversion to Christ.

". . .There are varieties of service," wrote St. Paul, "but the same Lord. . . .To each is given the manifestation of the Spirit for the common good" (I Corinthians 12:5, 7).

The traditional picture of an Episcopal parish is changing, but then again it has always been changing to admit new necessities and opportunities.

III. Church History

We might say that a fifth mark of an institution (see page 6 for first four marks) is its history, apart from which that institution cannot be understood. Christianity is a living and resilient religion. In this chapter I will present events in the history of the church which I believe to have been determinative not only in the past, but which present abiding issues confronting the church in every age.

The Church in Judaism

Judaism is our parent church. Those first Christians took with them part of the heritage of the synagogue. They called Jesus Messiah. Even the Christian year, with its cycle of festivals of faith, was related to the Jewish one.

The Old Testament Scriptures were basic to early Christian worship. Before the appearance of the letters of St. Paul, and before the appearance of the Gospels, the early Christians used Scriptures particularly prophetic of the appearance and ministry of Jesus.

The early Christians saw themselves as part of an on-going movement, the roots of which lay in God's revelation to the patriarchs and prophets. In a real sense, baptism dramatized the symbolic truth that the candidate was contemporary with those who fled Pharaoh. Jesus became the new Moses, his teachings new prophecy, although in fulfillment of priesthood and sacrifice.

In the seventh chapter of the Acts of the Apostles we find one of the most primitive summaries of the meaning of Old Testament history, as interpreted by the Christian community. The apostolic preaching found in the Acts is crucial toward understanding how the first Christians saw themselves.

St. Paul

St. Paul's letters are an invaluable source for understanding the early church. The Acts of the Apostles represent primary sources of his missionary journeys. He does not tell us much about himself except that he was unimpressive in appearance and not a good public speaker. He was afflicted by a mysterious disease which he called his "thorn in the flesh" (possibly epilepsy or malaria). He is important to us because his life reflects the conflicts of his time—the conflict between Judaism and the emerging church, between law and grace, between old tradition and new testimony.

His initiation into Christianity was not through a process of instruction from the apostles, but rather it came in a vision of the risen Christ, confronting him with the question, "Saul, Saul, why do you persecute me?" (Acts 26:12-18). At the time of this revelation he was on his way to Damascus to disperse a Christian church because he passionately believed that Christianity was a heretical deviant of the true faith of Judaism.

His conversion has been viewed clinically as a psychotic episode. It has been suggested that his militant zeal, coupled with a sense of doubt which lay deep within him about the rightness of what he was doing, created a projection on his part of the appearance of the one he was persecuting. There are variants of this theory, not only in regard to St. Paul, but in regard to others who have experienced dramatic conversion. One must point out, however, that psychologizing from a distance tends to produce neat and simplistic answers.

Whatever might be said of this kind of experience in the language of abnormal psychology, what we do see in St. Paul is a man gifted with remarkable leadership ability and the ability to cope with conflicts that could have destroyed the church. We cannot help but be impressed by his affirmation to Timothy, ". . . I know whom I have believed . . ." (II Timothy 1:12). What is significant about his experience is that it represented his call to be an apostle apart from the testimony of the other apostles. His credentials lay in his personal experience of the risen Lord.

While this kind of appeal to a private revelation has been traditionally mistrusted by those in positions of ecclesiastical authority (and sometimes with good reason), St. Paul offers a classic precedent for understanding the truth that God is not the property of a particular kind of ministerial succession. In Paul, God chose to use someone hostile as one of the primary missionaries of his church to his church, and to those outside of the church. As a former persecutor of the church, he was distrusted by the Christian communities he visited; but, because he was thoroughly conversant with the traditions of Judaism, he provided a theological understanding of the emergence of the church.

This was the first crucial issue the early church faced—the relationship between the old and new Israel. Was Christianity ("the way") a new institution and "covenant," setting forth a new history of salvation, or was it primarily an expression of a divergent Judaism? As Jesus was a Jew and kept the Law (capitalized, this means Jewish, not civil, law), to what extent were Christians obliged to honor and claim that tradition? Simply put, the question was, "Did one have to become a Jew to become a Christian?"

Those who answered "yes" recalled Jesus' saying that he had come not to destroy but to fulfill the Law. Thus those who had come into the Christian church from Judaism felt obliged to continue the rite of circumcision and to abstain from meats butchered in temples dedicated to pagan gods. Those who answered "no" were Gentiles or non-Jews. They favored such teachings of Jesus as "the sabbath was made for man and not man for the sabbath." They perceived Jesus to be casual in regard to the stringent demands of Judaism and saw no reason why their new life in Christ should be confined to Jewish legalism.

Out of this basic issue came the question of the relationship between law and grace. Paul's letters to the church in Galatia and to the church in Rome are crucial. He conceded that the Law had a positive value in the history of Israel. It ordered their community and protected them from assimilation into the religions surrounding them and pervading their culture. St. Paul viewed the Law as a "pedagogue," one who led a child to school and was responsible for him until he arrived. The Law, then, was preparatory, leading to the Messiah who would fulfill the Law, who would invest it with its true meaning.

The problem with the Law was twofold. First, it possessed significance only to those who were under it—the Jews. Second, and more crucial, there was a dangerous tendency on the part of those under it to trust in it as a means of their acceptance of "justification" by God. The Law in post-exilic Judaism had become so complex and subtle that there was often severe disagreement among the rabbis as to how it was to be applied. Thus, if keeping the Law had to do with one's salvation or "justification," then this meant trouble for those with neither the learning nor the leisure to meditate upon it.

Thus St. Paul viewed Law as necessarily preparatory and stabilizing, indeed as "righteous and holy." He did not perceive Jesus to be breaking it so much as fulfilling it in creative ways. For example, the healings done by Jesus on the Sabbath illustrated the breaking of the Law so that its real purpose might be fulfilled.

This interpretation on the part of St. Paul raises a serious question. If the Christian is to live beyond the Law, beyond legalism, how then does he order his life? How does one live responsibly in his new freedom without Law? Whereas Jewish Christians were intent upon trying to bring the Gentile Christians into the fold of the Law, in the name of celebrating their freedom from the Law some of the Gentiles were moving in the direction of license and immorality.

Theologically, this is called antinomianism—"against Law." In his letters to the church at Corinth, St. Paul dealt with several situations illustrative of this problem. One man was living in open adultery with his brother's wife. Another was openly eating meat sacrificed in pagan temples, scandalizing Jewish converts in the name of freedom from legalism.

Liberation from legalism has often been another name for antinomianism in the history of the church. It has been a continuing problem, sometimes manifested in religious communes where the institution of marriage was abandoned for a more "spiritual" mode of living. It has been manifested in the ignoring of discipline and standards, often proving that, as in the case of the prodigal son, newfound freedom can quickly lead to forms of bondage.

Its opposite—legalism—whether manifest in Catholic or Protestant traditions, has always been with us. Ironically, the Christian church, which was to have manifested a "new covenant" of grace and freedom, became in time highly institutionalized, reflective of the system from which it emerged. Institutions can drift either into antinomianism or legalism. For example, the Protestant Reformation, which had its immediate origin in Luther's experience of God's grace and forgiveness, his experience of "justification by faith," in time gave birth to a system of strict orthodoxy and legalism. At the time of the Protestant Reformation there were spin-off movements featuring antinomian tendencies, in reaction to both Protestant and Catholic traditions.

In the fifteenth chapter of the Acts of the Apostles, the church met in council to resolve the conflict between Jew and Gentile. The guidelines which emerged were: Those who had come into the church from Judaism were to be permitted to continue the traditions important to them but these traditions were not to be imposed upon Gentiles as standards. On the other hand, those who had no experience of what it meant to be a Jew were to refrain from doing in the name of freedom those things which scandalized the Jewish Christians.

St. Paul insisted that "neither circumcision counts for anything nor uncircumcision, but keeping the commandments of God" (I Corinthians 7:19). The invitation both to Jew and Gentile was to become "a new creature in Christ." Often the issues which impede denominational communion, as well as charity within a particular denomination, are issues which symbolically reflect circumcision and uncircumcision. Certainly, in the minds of many, it is difficult to distinguish between "the commandments of God" and the traditions to which we attach divine importance.

This issue is one of continuing importance to a church which exists for mission, a church addressing itself to cultures in which traditions vary. Two perspectives toward mission have been prominent in the history of the church. First, other religions are basically wrong and their adherents are heading for hell. This is what I call the "save-the-savage syndrome." Second, Christianity is essentially a religion congenial with humanitarian development of deprived cultures. We are sent not as apostles, but as doctors and technicians. This assumes that all religions are equally right and equally wrong.

But there is a third motive for mission which has characterized Anglicanism and churches in the Catholic tradition. While this motive embraces aspects of the first two mentioned, it is based primarily upon St. Paul's conviction that God has revealed himself in the conscience of all men. "When Gentiles who have not the law do by nature what the law requires, they are a law to themselves, even though they do not have the law" (Romans 2:14). It is stated in Colossians 1:15–20 that Christ "is the image of the invisible God . . . for in him all things were created . . . and in him all things hold together."

Catholic tradition assumes what has been called "natural theology," which recognizes that in mysterious ways God has been there ahead of his missionaries. The missionary bears the proclamation of salvation in Jesus. The doctrines of the Incarnation and the Atonement, unique to Christianity, answer the yearning, as no other religion can, of humanity for wholeness, peace, salvation, forgiveness of sin, and release from despair. Jesus is both Savior and Answer to our deepest questions. The coming of the magi or wise men described in St. Matthew's Gospel indicates the belief of the early church that before Jesus went to those beyond the pale of Palestine, the Gentile world, the world of pagan and "natural" religion came to him in the persons of the magi.

God alone is the judge of what lies in the conscience and in the hearts of men and women, who goes to heaven or hell. We believe that Christ completes the partiality of other religions and, in him, is salvation from the errors found in aspects of other religions.

Christian faith has been enriched by some of the traditions of the cultures to which it has come, but by the same token Christianity has assumed certain cultural values, standards of dress, etc., which have caused confusion and rejection in other cultures.

A remarkable fact about the Anglican Communion today is its rapid growth in Africa. By 1981 it is estimated that Uganda will have more Anglicans than are in the United States! It is my conviction that in significant measure the renewal of Western Christendom will come from those nations where we have sent missionaries so many years ago. The bread of life we cast upon the waters will come back to us.

St. Paul would have been astonished to have been told he was writing Scripture. What became Scripture were letters written because of the problems manifested in the young churches. These letters do not give us a systematic theology of St. Paul, a theology written in detachment, but a theology born of experience, of struggle with what is the tradition of men and what is the will of God.

The church has been shaped by those who have confronted the figure of St. Paul. To understand St. Augustine, Martin Luther, John Wesley, and Karl Barth, one must spend some time with St. Paul. The issues with which he wrestled are issues of faith in every generation. One of his lasting legacies was his insight:

> But now in Christ Jesus you who once were far off have been brought near in the blood of Christ. For he is our peace, who has made us both one, and has broken down the dividing wall of hostility, by abolishing in his flesh the law of commandments and ordinances, that he might create in himself one new man in place of the two, so making peace (Ephesians 2:13-15).

Conflict with the State

The first conflict the church faced was within its own family. Conflict centered in the meaning of "old" and "new" covenants, the role of Law, and whether Christianity was in reality a liberal sect of Judaism or a church in its own right.

The next conflict was with the state. The first Christians took literally Jesus' counsel to render under Caesar what is his and unto God what is his. The Acts of the Apostles, attributed to St. Luke, is an apologetic, a reasoned attempt to demonstrate that Christianity intended no subversion of the state and that most of the crises which emerged were usually precipitated by hostile Jews. Roman rule, extending as it did from Scotland to Persia, wisely permitted the existence of a variety of religions.

Toleration of religion did not mean, as far as the government was concerned, that there would be no formal allegiance to the cult of the emperor. One was free to have a personal faith as long as a visible allegiance to the religion of the state was periodically displayed. This religion centered in the person of the emperor, who represented the divine *Roma*. The peace and prosperity enjoyed by the citizens of the empire was considered to be supernaturally influenced; the gods watched over the empire as long as loyalty oaths were offered up before imperial images.

When Christianity emerged, Rome was already in a process of decay. As Powell Mills Dawley puts it, "The empire in the end worshipped itself to death."[1] The work of the invading tribes was made easier by the collapse of morality, patriotism, and economic stability. Along with these factors, there was an agnosticism, a cynical disbelief in the powers of the Roman gods, a sense of despair.

The church was the victim of an eleventh-hour attempt to save the empire. The misfortunes of the empire were linked in the mind of some emperors to the appearance of Christianity. The persecutions began under Nero, who blamed the Christians for the great fire in Rome in 64 A.D. The persecutions were to vary in severity and strategy. Some were aimed only at the leadership of the church. Some emperors in subtle ways tried to bribe leaders of the church by offering them governmental favors; other emperors simply set out to slaughter. The slogan of the government became, "It is not lawful for you to exist." Just as twentieth-century Jews experienced the Holocaust, so also did simply being a Christian mean death.

In spite of these systematic attempts to exterminate it, the church grew stronger. In a climate of uncertainty, Christians seemed to know in whom they believed. The early Christians did not possess the sophistication that was later to characterize some aspects of the church. In the chapel of Emperor Alexander Severus were statues of Greek gods, a statue of Abraham, the statues of some philosophers, and even one of Jesus! The proclamation of Peter in the Acts of the Apostles—"There is no other name given unto us under Heaven whereby we may be saved"—was the rallying cry of the first Christians.

The persecution under Decius was characterized by the attempt of the government to make it easy to secure certificates proving that an individual or family had offered sacrifice, thus providing exemption from persecution. The government wisely realized, as some totalitarian governments do today, that division in the church was an effective means of weakening it, and that, by making it easy to comply with civil decrees, division could easily be created.

The result of this Roman approach nearly accomplished what prior persecutions had failed to. Many complied with the state and continued to receive the sacraments. They reasoned that, because they did not believe in what the pinch of incense meant, what difference did it make if they did it crossing their fingers spiritually?

At the end of the reign of Decius, a forty-year period of peace followed; but there was no peace within the church. A priest named Novatian represented a faction of Christians who had endured persecution without compromise. They were opposed to the lenient treatment of those priests and laity who had betrayed Christian discipline, yet still received the sacraments of the church. Novatian and his followers left the church, as did a priest by the name of Donatus some years later. Both Novatian and Donatus believed that the church had to remain a community of the "faithful." Donatus maintained that any priest or bishop who showed leniency toward the lapsed, or lapsed himself, was no longer entitled to administer a valid sacrament.

This issue was to arise again and again throughout the history of the church. Names changed, but the principles at stake remained the same. Is the church to be constituted only by the faithful, representing a "pure" society consisting of those who have proven themselves? Or is the church to be representative of those whose faith, like Peter's, was weak at a crucial time. Are there to be tares among the wheat?

The Catholic Church gradually emerged as the name given to the mainline expression of Christian faith. St. Augustine was its most eloquent spokesman during this time, insisting that confession and absolution were given to the church for the purposes of restoration of the lapsed. The Catholic position is reflected in Article twenty-six of the Thirty-Nine Articles in the Prayer Book. That article begins by noting, "Although in the visible Church the evil be ever mingled with the good. . . . Neither is the effect of Christ's ordinance taken away by their wickedness, . ." (that is, the wickedness of certain clergy).

Catholic doctrine holds that, regardless of the personal immorality or morality of the priest at the time of the administration of a sacrament, the sacrament is valid because it is Christ's sacrament, bearing his promise and presence.

The Puritan movement in the seventeenth century reflects the views of Novatian and Donatus. The practice of some denominations to vote on membership along with the obsession with preserving pure doctrine indicates that this issue is still alive, as is the issue of law and grace, and the issue of the Christian's loyalty to the state when the latter does not permit acts of conscience or freedoms which should be maintained.

Gnosticism

Persecution tends to create affirmation of faith. What nearly destroyed the church was the subtle infiltration of its faith by elements of pagan philosophy, introduced into the church by converts from various cults. Many of these wanted to interpret Christian faith in terms of philosophical speculation and mythologies.

The Mediterranean world was filled with a multitude of cults, mythologies, and philosophies, along with exotic rituals which offered answers to the deepest questions and anxieties of men and women. The expansion of Christianity brought it into competitive contact with Gnosticism.

Gnosticism (from the Greek word *gnosis,* "knowledge") is a term that historians of religion use to describe a collection of speculative philosophies and theologies which, although differing in detail, rests upon the assumption that a secret system of knowledge existed; it was given to the apostles covertly and was not for public distribution. The literature of Gnosticism is varied and fantastic, but there are common threads binding it together. The primary emphasis was on an esoteric revelation given to enlighten the apostles.

The myths of Gnosticism affirmed an original heaven or pleroma, representing the habitation of all spiritual reality. This heaven had blown apart at one time and fragments of its spirituality drifted into the dark abyss where matter existed. Between heaven (where all true spirituality is located) and earth, there were gradations of spiritual reality. All Gnostics agreed that good and evil were perpetually at war. Evil was inherent in creation and matter. Thus salvation meant the release of the imprisoned spiritual spark from the body, to wind its way upward from matter, the property of Satan, to its true home.

The world, according to Gnosticism, was created by an evil being, or demiurge. Christ came to free us from an evil world under control of the demiurge. By definition Jesus could not have had a physical body. His humanity was only apparent, not real. His death on the cross was staged to provide an illusion of death. This heresy is called Docetism, from a Greek word which means to "appear" or to "seem." The Docetists created a collection of Scripture, Gnostic in nature.

According to the Gnostics, man was not a victim of sin or the consequences of his willful acts, but rather was a victim of unenlightenment.

Salvation was primarily a matter of knowledge through meditation and varying types of cleansing ritual. Again, this knowledge was not for all, but for the few gifted with spiritual comprehension.

In time Gnostic gospels began to appear—the *Gospel of Philip,* the *Gospel of Mary,* the *Wisdom of Faith,* the *Dialogue of the Savior,* the *Gospel of Thomas,* to name but a few. The Scriptures which constitute our present Bible represent the response of the Catholic Church to Gnostic gospels and teaching.

Along with the formation of the Catholic canon or standard of Scripture, there emerged an emphasis upon the importance of apostolic succession, the need to be in communion with teaching derived from orthodox bishops whose line of succession originated with the apostles. These gave stability to many who were confused by Gnostic speculation.

In our day there has been a renewed search for the sacred and the spiritual. Astrology and the occult represent a kind of Gnostic quest for a knowledge of the unseen. In some measure the church shares some responsibility for the emergence of these movements in that the emphasis upon social action, important as that is, can preempt our hunger for the spiritual.

The emphasis upon "secular Christianity" (the word secular is derived from the Latin, meaning "of this age") rightly sets before us that creation is good and that "God so loved the world that he sent his only begotten son. . . . " The scenario of our redemption takes place in the world. A persistent temptation of the church, however, is to ally itself with secularism and thus to experience seduction by the power structures of the world. The church can lose its soul while trying to gain power, prestige, and relevance.

In our computer-crafted culture in which science, technology, and rationalism have left the imagination of many with no place to go, we note the appearance of the literature of fantasy, the popularity of nostalgia, and techniques of meditation imported from Eastern religions.

Christian faith is rich in mysticism and varying opportunities of spirituality. The spirituality of St. John's Gospel has no peer in the literature of spirituality, for here, as indeed in all of the Gospels, we experience a Lord who celebrates the good things of creation—bread, wine, laughter, and the realities of nature.

Our liturgy celebrates the presence of "things unseen"—"angels, archangels, and all the company of heaven." Gnosticism presumes to tell us far more about these realities than church Scripture reveals. It is impressive to note that Jesus, the most spiritual of all men, spent little time in speculations on the spiritual.

As the author of II Peter puts it, "For we did not follow cleverly devised myths when we made known to you the power and coming of our Lord Jesus Christ..." (II Peter 1:16).

Constantine

In 311 A.D. the Emperor Galarius promulgated the Edict of Toleration, which meant that Christianity was legally recognized by the state. When Constantine came to power, the state of the church became the church of the state. At the battle of Mulvian Bridge Constantine is reported to have seen a cross in the sky which bore the motto "by this sign you shall conquer."

Constantine saw in the church what succeeding emperors were to see, a means to unify the empire. Constantine became both convert and patron, which meant competing religions were put at a disadvantage. Upon his deathbed, he was baptized, laying aside his imperial robes for the simple white garment. Constantine believed, as many did in his time, that sins committed after baptism were not subject to forgiveness.

It has been observed that the legalization of the church was the occasion for its downfall, that its strongest witness came in times of persecution. Patronage and privilege are not necessarily conducive to spiritual health. The result of this is reflected in the conflicts which were to come in later years between bishop and king.

The positive side of this is reflected in the fact that Christian morality and teaching began to permeate the empire. Barbarian tribes, sweeping into the empire, in time were conquered by the church. A crumbling empire was ready for a new God for its old ones were dead or dying.

The Church in the Middle Ages

In the fifth and sixth centuries Germanic tribes moved into Roman provinces. In many cases these invading tribes were quietly assimilated. As civil stability gave way, the administrative ability of bishops like St. Ambrose of Milan provided leadership which was at once temporal and spiritual. When the Emperor Theodosius I summarily executed seven thousand citizens of Thessalonica (where the governer had been murdered in a revolt), Ambrose excommunicated the emperor until he submitted to penitential discipline. A precedent was set for ecclesiastical and political relationships.

Like others after him, Ambrose considered the church and state to have their respective autonomies. It was the duty of the Christian emperor to support and protect the church, and to issue legislation in accord with Christian principles.

St. Augustine, in his classic *The City of God*, gave this concept its most dramatic literary shape. As noted, he confronted the Donatists, but he also engaged in debate with a British monk by the name of Pelagius, who taught that salvation lay in self-initiative and good works, and that man was essentially good. Augustine spoke the mind of the church against the persistent presupposition that man in and of himself through his works can attain salvation. A good example of Pelagianism is the popular statement, "God helps those who help themselves."

Augustine answered the accusation of many pagans that the fall of the empire was due to the church. He affirmed the existence of two communities, one representing the civil powers and the other representing the spiritual community of the faithful. Although man is a citizen of an earthly city, his true citizenship is in the City of God. This concept is integral to the thought of the Middle Ages.

The Western and Eastern Churches

In 330 A.D. Constantine made the Greek city of Byzantium the capital of the empire and renamed it Constantinople. It remained the capital of the eastern section of the empire until 1453. Both Rome and Constantinople became powerful centers of the church, each with its peculiar expressions of theological definitions of the faith and each with different ways of looking at the relationship between church and state.

From the early Middle Ages on, the bishop of Rome became regarded more and more as the spokesman for the Western church. He had inherited the mantle of the Caesars and, in the vacuum created by the collapse of civil government, he came to exercise great powers, both political and religious.

Latin was the language of the West and Greek the language of the East. The Latin church interpreted itself to be the visible expression of the City of God; the state existed to carry out its decrees and to protect it. In the East, however, the emperor was considered to be the "head" of the church. There was little or no concept of the separation of powers, the delineation of sacred and secular. This concept, called caesaropapism, had a most notable Western representive centuries later in the person of Henry VIII.

In 1054 there was a formal split between the churches in communion with Rome and those in communion with Constantinople. This split was occasioned by their respective attitudes regarding the role of church and state. But behind this there were cultural differences which had long been present. The Eastern church tended to express its thought in mystical terms. Its piety was otherworldly. The Western church tended to express its faith in terms of the legal heritage derived from Roman law.

The Rise of the Papacy

As noted, one of the legacies left to the church by the Caesars was the heritage of law, the love of systematic thought. Tertullian provides a significant example of this. A student of law in Rome, upon his conversion he applied his learning to the task of systematic theology. He was the first in a succession of theologians in the West to bring to Christian doctrine a sense of precision and clarity.

Powell Mills Dawley summarizes three aspects of the Christian institution which led to its success in creating a Christian civilization in Europe: (1) "A controlling sense of Christian stewardship," by which he means that all possessions and talents were related to service of God; (2) "An effective moral power," which refers to the ethical life defined by the church; (3) "The independence of the spiritual life," which means that no civil powers had the right to interfere with one's faith (unless it were non-Christian).[2]

In 800 A.D., on Christmas Day, Charlemagne was crowned Holy Roman Emperor by the pope. This dramatized the assumption that the Bishop of Rome was the effective president and chief pastor. By a gradual process Rome came to be viewed as the spiritual center of the Western church, defining faith and ecclesiastical policy.

A great deal of this authority rested upon the stability of Rome and the organizational ability of popes. Gradually, however, the papacy read into its existence divine intent. As Rome had presumably been the place of Peter's martyrdom, he who was the "rock" of the church (Matthew 16:13-20), the bishops of Rome came to see themselves as "Vicars of Christ" upon the earth.

Although the doctrine of papal infallibility was not officially promulgated until the first Vatican Council of 1870, the foundations of this doctrine were laid in the pronouncements of such popes as Gregory I, Nicholas I, Gregory VII and, most dramatically, Innocent III. A refreshing note of pastoral servanthood was characterized by the reign of Gregory I in the seventh century, and manifested by the gentle John XXIII and the present pope, John Paul II.

In the Middle Ages a classic controversy emerged in regard to the respective powers of pope and king. As one pope put it, the church was the sun and civil powers were lesser lights. The logic of this led to the investiture controversies which centered in the issue of who had the right to appoint and invest bishops with their symbols of office. This was most dramatically illustrated in the excommunication of Henry IV of Germany by Pope Gregory VII. Henry had presumed to invest his bishops with their symbols of office. Because the pope had released the subjects of Henry from obedience to their king, popular pressure brought Henry to his knees in the snow in front of the pope's residence at Canossa, whereupon he received forgiveness and restoration. However, this event signaled one of the last instances of this kind of papal authoritarianism.

In the later Middle Ages attempts were made to hold councils of the church where representatives of the clergy and laity worked out mediating possibilities between papal authoritarianism and the authoritarianism of civil authorities. These attempts, called conciliarism, largely met with failure. The Second Vatican Council in our time was representative of some of the hopes of these councils, pressing as it did for collegiate sharing of authority by bishops and pope, and setting forth ministries of the laity.

Monasticism

The early Middle Ages in Western Europe were deemed the "dark ages" for several reasons: the presence of superstition, the "worldliness" of the church, and general intellectual stagnation.

The monastic life, however, represents a bright spot, and illustrates the truth that ecclesiastical authority cannot for long hold together the institution apart from the presence of spiritual realities which have the power to capture the human heart and mind.

The word *monasticism* comes from the Latin meaning "one." In the second century one man, Anthony, led thousands into the deserts of Egypt to lead solitary lives of contemplation. In time, individuals began to form communities. Some were primarily defined by an emphasis on contemplation. Others emphasized study and teaching, along with farming. In varying ways they all incorporated worship, prayer, and work.

Thus, very early in its history the church recognized the need to provide a style of life for those who wanted to adhere closely to the life of Jesus. The problem, then, as now, was how to maintain the spiritual life in an increasingly secular world. What is the nature of "total commitment" to Christ? For many, monasticism did and still does provide a way of realizing the Christian vocation. The monasteries provided a place for vocation—the calling not only to a life of prayer, worship, and study, but in the Middle Ages a place where one could copy the Scriptures, thus ensuring their perpetuation.

The Protestant Reformers tended to repudiate the monastic life because monasticism had become an institution bent upon the acquisition of property and power. At the time of the Reformation nearly a third of England belonged to monastic orders.

Protestantism has traditionally distrusted monasticism as the more "perfect" way. Luther and his followers rightly emphasized the need to follow Christ by participation in secular society (as did St. Francis of Assisi). The writings of Dietrich Bonhoeffer, martyred by the Nazis, center on the theme of "holy worldliness," engagement rather than retreat.

The monastic life, however, is unfairly viewed solely as retreat or escape. The Protestant monastery in Taize, France, for example, provides opportunities for clergy and laity to refresh themselves spiritually, to learn ways of meditation so that they can become effective mediators of the gospel. To pray is to work. To contemplate is an active offering of our spiritual nature. To learn to be still is to discover the activity of God within us. Intercession is involvement and ministry.

What We Have Inherited from the Middle Ages

The architecture of many of our churches reflects the abiding influence of the Middle Ages. Although, at the time of its appearance, Rome denounced Gothic architecture as barbaric and inconsistent with the "Romanesque" tradition, Gothic architecture came to symbolize for millions the expression of the "holy." Its vaulted arches proclaim a sense of transcendence, the majesty of God.

In contrast to Gothic architecture, much of contemporary church architecture, with its freestanding altars and churches in the round, expresses the concept of community, the belief that God is. in our midst, that he is to be encountered in community. Contemporary architecture captures something of the worship life of the early church, especially with the presence of the freestanding altar.

The altars and rood screens of Gothic tradition testify to the importance of awe and mystery to worship. A folk mass celebrated around a table and a solemn High Mass with medieval plainsong and incense both witness to truths important to worship. We can and do have both.

The church of the Middle Ages fused art and music in the worship of God. The medieval church offered some abiding insights, chief of which is that the whole of human creativity can be offered to God and become signs of his presence. The building of a medieval church was at once the building of a community which employed a diversity of talents.

Medieval man might not have been able to articulate theologically the relationship of God to the world, but he experienced a sense of the holy because his life was surrounded by symbolism. The shadow of the church fell across his comings and goings.

Just as artisans in wood, stone, and glass created cathedrals, so also there were those who created theological structures of faith. St. Anselm approached the task of theology by his assertion *credo ut intelligam* ("I believe in order that I might understand"). Peter Abelard stated the reverse: "I understand in order that I may believe." Abelard set a precedent with far-reaching implications in the history of philosophy by refusing to base his faith upon the uncritical examination of what had been handed down to him.

St. Thomas Aquinas was the preeminent theologian of the Middle Ages. His intellectual enterprise is in its own way a Gothic cathedral of thought, a systematic presentation of doctrine which earned him the title "the angelic doctor." While one might disagree with his method, or accept it only in part, the implications of his system cannot be taken lightly. Aquinas sought to incorporate two realities of our experience—reason and faith. He was indebted to Aristotle, who gave philosophy a scientific method. Aristotle demonstrated that it was both possible and necessary to think rationally about the world.

As we mentioned earlier, St. Paul believed, on the basis of Stoic philosophy, that all men had received "natural" revelation (Acts 17:22-32). The proofs of God's existence, according to Aquinas, can be perceived in the design of creation by the fact that creation had to be set in motion, that there was some "first cause."

On the other hand, although we may reasonably suppose that God exists because there is design and order in the universe, we have no way of knowing what this creator is like until he chooses to reveal himself.

To accept the revelation given in Scripture requires an act of faith, whereas the idea of a "prime mover" is a reasonable one. The meaning of life, its destiny and purpose, is given definition in the life and teachings of Jesus Christ, appropriated by faith.

One does not have to be a theologian and philosopher to grasp the truth that we are creatures capable of, indeed dependent upon, the exercise of faith and reason. Inevitably, we raise the question of how we come to know and believe in certain realities and not others, how we verify our assumptions. Nor are we exempt from the question which involves our dependence upon revelation, our need for faith: What is the good life? Why are some experiences more meaningful than others? Can we prove or demonstrate these qualities in advance?

Perhaps the first question in our life is that of the child—Who made God? As we mature, we are confronted by experiences which raise the question of God's existence and his caring for us. We confront the problems of despair and hope. If we choose to remain apart from Christian faith, we must necessarily come to terms with what values, principles, and standards are required to sustain some sort of sane and reasonably happy existence. Faith and reason are necessary to human existence in that they claim the purposes for which we live.

A couple may come to me for marriage claiming they are in love. Following premarital counseling involving compatibility tests, however, their commitment "until we are parted by death" is a faith commitment, both to each other and to God.

The Judeo-Christian faith rests upon God's calling Abraham from his homeland and making promises to him incapable of verification in advance. Abraham is willing to surrender and to risk faith.

In my pilgrimage in faith I have come to believe that it is not unfaithful to have reason nor is it unreasonable to have faith. This is not only at the heart of the great theological systems but is at the heart of life itself.

IV. The Church of England

The Early British Church

The apocryphal Acts of Pilate and the Life of Joseph of Arimathea attest to traditions which claim that Joseph, after being arrested for his role in the burial of Jesus, was released and commissioned by the apostle Philip to visit England in 63 A.D. Some legends claim that St. Paul was in England around 64 A.D. and that Joseph of Arimathea was the founder of Glastonbury Abbey. (This speculation has its basis in the works of Baronius, a sixteenth-century historian.) We do know that by the end of the second century Christians were in England.

By the time of St. Paul's missionary journeys, Rome had subjugated the Celts, natives of Britannia. By 175 A.D., Christianity was taking root in Britannia because of influences from Europe. While much of the history of the early Christian communities is obscure, from the early part of the fourth century some solid information is available. St. Augustine, as we said earlier, debated Pelagius, a British monk. Churchmen from Britain were in attendance at the council called by Constantine in Arles in 314 A.D. During the last imperial persecution Alban, a Roman soldier, was martyred for hiding a priest. He confessed to being a Christian and became a popular saint among the British people.

Following this period, barbarian hordes descended upon the Empire. The Angles and Saxons swept into England, and the British church was dispersed into Wales and Scotland. A veil of paganism fell upon the country.

Missionaries from Rome

By the latter part of the sixth century, Rome was engaged in the conversion of those tribes that had overrun the empire. The Franks in

Gaul had been "converted" (in those days the conversion of entire peoples was often forced upon them by the sword of their converted kings).

Pope Gregory I sent a mission to England under the leadership of Augustine. Following the conversion of King Ethelbert, a church was founded at Canterbury which became a base for missions. It was Pope Gregory's intent that the experience of conversion be accompanied by reverence for Roman authority. The Celtic Christians, alienated from the Anglo-Saxons, had practiced their faith in isolation. They were in no mood to hear abut loyalty to Rome.

The Celtic Christians in Ireland, under the leadership of St. Patrick, manifested an intense sense of mission. Scotland and the islands to the west of England were objects of their missions. St. Columba founded a Christian community at Iona in 563. He is another great figure in the history of missionary activity. Augustine's missionaries made their way to the north and met the Celtic missionaries on their way south from Scotland. The critical issue facing them was to whom they should give their allegiance—to the pope and the Roman church or to their own loosely knit but effective confederacy centered at Iona.

A crucial event in the history of the English church was the Synod of Whitby in 664 A.D. Here extensive debate centered upon the differences between Roman and Celtic customs. Although the issues seem trivial enough to us, they were important to those assembled. One issue concerned the date of Easter. Another had to do with the tonsure, the proper cut of the clergy's hair.

However, the underlying issue had to do with where, in the future, authority in these matters and others should be found. To be Catholic meant to multitudes the necessity of following the directives and customs of Roman Christendom. The decision was made in favor of Rome. Perhaps this was the wise move, for it brought England into the mainstream of those forces shaping a common faith all over Europe.

The English church, from the Synod of Whitby until the coming of William the Conqueror, experienced a gradual evolution into the shape of a national church. Under men like Archbishop Theodore of Canterbury, monasticism was given new life and the diocesan structure came into existence. Gradually, the Saxon church, inspired by the heritage of Celtic devotion, entered upon a missionary thrust. St. Boniface, a Saxon, and St. Willibrord engaged in a European mission, thus indicating the ability of English Christianity to go beyond its national boundaries.

The Norman invasion brought England into a more intimate relation with Continental influences. Norman architecture, characterized by its circular arches and fortresslike appearance, became the standard. The Norman invasion also meant the transformation of the English bishop into a feudal lord, resembling his counterpart on the Continent. This was the age of feudalism, with its hierarchy and system of vassalage. Bishops and abbots of monastic houses became part of the system, rendering loyalty to those who gave them their vast holdings and privileges.

During this period the promulgation of extensive ecclesiastical laws came about. If the state had its civil code of "common law," the church also expected to legislate in matters of faith and religious discipline. Although William I separated the royal courts from the ecclesiastical courts, it was often difficult to separate the spiritual from the secular. The church concerned itself with concerns which to many of us today would seem more properly to belong to the state—divorce, contested wills, drunkenness, adultery, and questionable business practices.

Henry II and Thomas Becket

Thus the feudal system was characterized by a double loyalty. The bishop was at once an apostolic man and a feudal baron. The manner of the selection and investiture of bishops dramatized recurring conflict between the claims of the papacy and those of royal powers. A compromise of sorts was reached whereby the bishop would show homage to the king who would invest him with his holdings. The church, through its representation, would give the bishop his staff and ring, symbolizing his spiritual authority. This arrangement essentially avoided the seemingly insoluble question of whose power was the greater.

The murder of Thomas Becket at the hands of the knights of Henry II foreshadowed the conflict which was to come between Henry VIII and the pope. Becket insisted that clergy convicted of crimes were to be disciplined only by ecclesiastical courts; Henry insisted on their being turned over to the royal courts following sentencing by church courts.

Becket claimed that this was trying a person twice for the same crime. Becket also resented Henry's policy of shutting off appeals to Rome without his permission and the king's arrogant assumption of the power to make appointments to bishoprics without consultation with ecclesiastical authorities. Becket proclaimed what he believed to be the truth—that kings receive their power and authority from the church.

The murder of Thomas Becket made him a martyr. Popular revulsion in the wake of this forced Henry II to do penance at the shrine of Thomas. Papal prestige peaked. Four hundred years later, Henry VIII was to reverse this scenario. Dr. Dawly observes: "If the plundering and destruction of the great shrine of St. Thomas Becket of Canterbury was one of the least admirable acts of Henry VIII, at least it indicated that monarch had some historical knowledge.[1]

Henry VIII

Although Henry VIII has been credited with founding the Church of England, in reality he nationalized the church which had been in England from early times. He nationalized and reconstituted a church composed of Celtic, Saxon and Roman influences.

As we have noted, the history of the church in England was characterized by the unresolved conflict between pope and crown. While the English church and crown were willing to accept the pope as the spiritual head of the church, taxes levied by Rome against the English church proved to be a cause of mounting anger and restlessness.

The pope's refusal to permit Henry's divorce from Catherine simply was a climax to what had been festering for a long time. His desire to marry Anne Boleyn was not an unreasonable one, given Catherine's inability to provide him with a male heir. Popes and bishops frequently annulled marriages for this reason.

The reason for refusal of Henry's annulment lay not with religious principles so much as political ones. Pope Clement VII was virtually a prisoner in Rome, surrounded by the imperial forces of Charles V, nephew of Catherine of Aragon. The pope was hardly in a position to render Henry a favorable judgment. Incidentally, it was Pope Julius who had set aside church law so that Henry could marry Catherine, who had been the wife of Henry's deceased brother Arthur. Such marriages were traditionally prohibited.

Henry's ultimate response was to pressure Parliament into removing the English church from its position of obedience to Rome. He then appropriated the vast holdings of the monastic houses. Unfortunately, these seizures were accompanied by senseless despoiling.

It is rather pointless to call either party in this conflict right or wrong. It dramatizes what was happening all over Europe. These were times when popes acted like kings and kings like popes. These people would have been astounded by the relatively modern concept of the separation of church and state.

Henry considered himself a theologian of note. He wrote a series of treatises denouncing the heresies of Protestantism, doing all in his power to keep the English church free from Lutheran and Calvinistic influences. For his efforts he was given the title "Defender of the Faith" by Pope Leo X, a title still preserved by English monarchs.

Henry believed, like many Englishmen before and after him, that to be a Catholic did not mean one had to subscribe to the doctrine of papal supremacy. Although he brought the English church under the authority of Parliament, he preserved the essentials of Catholic faith and worship, the historic ministry of bishops, priests, and deacons. He did permit the creed, the Lord's Prayer, and the Ten Commandments to be translated into English. Although the English church was influenced by the Protestant Reformation, then raging on the Continent, England was not destined to become a country of the church of the Reformation.

The Protestant Reformation

Historians have noted a variety of causes of the Protestant Reformation—the emergence of nationalism, the rise of commerce, the spread of learning. Certainly all of these created an atmosphere in which the Protestant Reformation could succeed where similar movements before it had failed.

This movement was inspired and given direction by Martin Luther, an Augustinian monk (although he was preceded by men like John Huss who shared similar concerns). Luther experienced a tormenting uncertainty, an anxiety in regard to his inability to feel forgiveness and to find reconciliation with a God, presumably gracious and forgiving. Although the Roman Catholic Church provided him with the traditional means of grace—prayer, fasting, and pilgrimages—no inner assurance was to be found. Like Wesley after him and others after Wesley, he discovered in St. Paul's letter to the church at Rome the clue to his problem. He had been trying meritoriously to earn God's forgiveness, when in reality it had been given and all he needed to do was to claim it in faith.

The Roman Catholic Church of his day had imposed an elaborate penitential system upon the faithful. Given the Latin love of legality, it was a brilliant system. In essence, it was grounded in the belief that Christ's obedience created an abundance of merit which could be applied to all who availed themselves of the system. The saints, by their good works, provided a deposit, indeed, a surplus of merit. The key to these treasures was held by the church. Particularly offensive to

Luther, as it was to many others, was the system of indulgences. These were certificates which could be purchased by the faithful and which would guarantee Masses to be said for them to shorten purgatorial pain. Luther also strongly believed that the Bible should be available in the language of the people. There has always been a tendency to falsely ascribe to Luther the belief that private interpretation was desirable. Luther believed that the Bible was the book of the church, and he was active in promoting persecution of revolutionary groups (the peasant's revolt) who based their actions on what they believed to be warranted by Scripture. There was no egalitarianism in Luther's teachings, as witnessed by his alliance with royal power against the peasant uprisings. In large measure, Luther's success was due to the patronage given him by the Emperor Frederick who, although no Henry VIII in theological matters, agreed with Henry as to the suffocating presence of the Roman church in German matters.

In fairness to the Roman Catholic Church, often painted the villain, there were those who preceded Luther, devout Catholics, who believed the church, particularly the institution of the papacy, needed reform. Although there is a sense in which conciliarism foreshadowed some of the reforms which occurred in the previous decade, the primary purpose of the Councils of Pisa (1409) and Constance (1414) was to bring to an end the argument of which of the three competing popes was to reign. The Council of Constance declared that its authority rested in Christ and that all orders of clergy, including the pope, and the laity were bound to obey its voice. Upon his election, Pope Martin V proceeded to denounce the council. He and his successors insisted even more rigidly upon their divine right of rule. The failure of the conciliar movement was a factor precipitating the Protestant Reformation.

The conciliar movement affirmed the standards of faith and doctrine as set forth by the great councils of the first five centuries before the emergence of papal claims to infallibility. Anglicans and the Orthodox value as standards of faith the promulgations of the church before its division in 1054.

No account of the Reformation is complete without mention of John Calvin. Like Tertullian, he was trained as a lawyer. In Geneva, where he settled, he composed his *Institutes of the Christian Religion,* a classic compendium offering the most systematic structure of Christian thought to emerge from the Protestant perspective. It is Protestantism's counterpart to the *Summa Theologica* of St. Thomas Aquinas. Calvin tried to model Geneva upon what he believed was the biblical order of a city. Not noted for his tolerance, he sentenced Serve-tus, who presumably denied the Trinity, to death at the stake.

Luther, Calvin, and Henry VIII, as well as the princes of the Roman Catholic Church, held at least one thing in common, that there could be no plurality of denominations existing in the same state. One of the outcomes of the Thirty Years War was the principle that a Christian was obliged to be a member of the denomination which existed in his particular state. The Anabaptists (so called because they believed in adult or believers' baptism) were persecuted by Catholic and Protestant alike, often being put to death by drowning as an ironic commentary on their own doctrine.

The Protestant Reformation precipitated what is called the Counter-Reformation of the Roman Catholic Church. The Jesuit order ("the pope's hounds") was dedicated to a militant loyalty to the pope and the promotion of Catholic teaching. Ironically, in our own times some leading Jesuit theologians have come to represent liberal voices in the church. Hans Küng has even questioned papal infallibility.

Any institution threatened by schism tends to become reactive. The Counter-Reformation led to a militant and defensive posture on the part of the Roman Catholic Church not wholly characteristic of it prior to the Protestant Reformation. There also emerged systems of Protestant orthodoxy and confessions of faith characterized by extreme rigidity, aimed both at Roman Catholicism and separatist churches who claimed they were under direct inspiration of the Holy Spirit and needed no traditional forms of ecclesiastical authority.

Ecumenical progress has been aided in our own time by the realization that our reactive postures have been occasioned not so much by doctrinal disagreement as by historical circumstance, the tendency to defend ourselves against each other. The Consultation on Church Union, primarily Protestant, and official conversations between and among Lutherans, Anglicans, Orthodox, and Roman Catholics, characterize our times.

Further Developments in England

Following the death of Henry VIII, Protestantism dominated the Church of England under the boy-king Edward VI. His protectors, the Dukes of Somerset and Northumberland, were avid proponents of the Reformation. The Prayer Book issued during Edward's reign reflects those sympathies.

Under Mary Tudor ("Bloody Mary") the English church was

brought back into the Roman orbit and then, under Elizabeth I, the church was once again established apart from papal control. In both of these reigns we observe churchmen of high and low rank dying for their respective loyalties.

Elizabeth's reign is of particular significance in that, in her time, the Church of England received its definitive position as a bridge church, or *via media*, which offered refuge from the alternatives of Roman Catholicism and Protestantism. The "Elizabethan Settlement" envisioned a church that could be for and of the English people. The Thirty-Nine Articles appended to our Prayer Book represent a doctrinal concensus upon which that church rested. Richard Hooker composed his *Ecclesiastical Polity*, a classic and definitive statement of Anglican theology in regard to the government of the church. John Jewel's *Apology for the Church of England* is another work of great importance. These works offer systematic expositions of what it means to be an Anglican.

Under James I, the King James Version (or Authorized Version) of the Bible appeared. Under Charles I, civil war erupted. Oliver Cromwell, the leader of the insurrection, was a militant Puritan opposed to episcopacy and its liaison with royal succession and its doctrine of divine right. Believing that divine right could work both ways, he proceeded to execute Archbishop Laud as well as Charles I. Episcopacy was formally abolished and Cromwell's Protectorate was its eminently Protestant replacement. Just as Archbishop Laud had imposed severe penalities upon those clergy with Puritan proclivities, so Cromwell returned the compliment.

The Puritans, many of whom fled to America, were so called because they wanted to restore "pure" doctrine to the church. Pure doctrine meant, among other things, churches without altars and stained glass, no rings at weddings, no kneeling for prayers, and a particular tonsure called "roundhead" because of its bowl-shaped appearance. There were to be no sports or sexual intercourse on Sunday. What we have come to call Sunday "blue laws" had their origin in Puritanism, which viewed the Sabbath largely in Jewish terms.

Following the regime of Cromwell, the monarchy was restored and Charles II, came to the throne; with him came the re-establishment of episcopacy. Both Puritans and Roman Catholics who did not conform were once again subjected to penalties. In fact it was not until 1829 that Roman Catholics were allowed to vote.

The English church has been shaped and defined by Protestant and Roman Catholic pressures. The Church of England has steadfastly refused to call itself Protestant in the traditional sense. But according to the literal meaning of the word—*pro testis,* "to testify for"—the Church of England is protestant. It has testified to and borne witness to the ancient order and faith of the church, enshrined in creed, sacrament, and apostolic succession. The Church of England has protested the identification of Catholicism as relating only to the Roman Catholic Church.

The Church of England has always held to the position that it is possible to assimilate the positive contributions of some of the aspects of the Protestant Reformation without becoming a Protestant church. It has asserted that it is not only possible but necessary to claim a Catholic heritage.

In essence then, the preceding discussion in this chapter shows that the three sources or streams which make up Anglicanism are:

(1) The Celtic church, characterized by its sense of mission and scholarship which influenced Saxon culture.

(2) The medieval Roman Catholic Church, which opened England to Continental influences and provided a center of unity in the papacy and the creeds of the historic church councils.

(3) The Protestant Reformation, which introduced the conviction as to the primacy of Scripture and the evangelical doctrine of "justification by faith."

The Episcopal Church in the United States

Elizabeth's reign witnessed the first English presence in America. The first known use of the Prayer Book in the New World was on the flagship of Sir Francis Drake off the coast of San Francisco in 1579. Some time later a priest named Thomas Hariot read the Bible to the Indians of Roanoke Island, and in 1587 baptism was administered for the first time in the English language on the Atlantic Coast. An Indian by the name of Manteo was the first convert in the new country and Virginia Dare, the first child born of English parents in America, was baptized.

In 1606 King James chartered the Virginia Company and in 1607 the Reverend Robert Hunt administered the sacraments to the Jamestown settlers. Hostile Indians and famine almost caused the extinction of the colony. An expedition by Lord Delaware revived the colony and the governors Sir Thomas Gates and Sir Thomas Dale furthered progress. There were setbacks—another massacre by the Indians in 1622, which led to the abandoning of an Indian mission and a university—but, by this time, the church was very much a part of life in the colony.

At the same time, the New England Puritans had their colonies and congregational churches. The Massachusetts Bay Colony was ordered along the lines of Calvin's concepts of an ideal community. This meant, of course, that the Prayer Book was forbidden and those who sympathized with episcopacy were unwelcome.

In America, as in Europe, the idea of toleration of dissent was not in vogue. The Episcopal Church in Virginia represented an establishment in one way, whereas the Puritan churches in New England represented another kind of establishment.

Between these establishments there was some moderation. Maryland offers a good example. Roman Catholics settled Maryland and, under the influence of Lord Baltimore, toleration was encouraged. The Episcopal Church was established in Georgia in 1758, but its growth was slow compared to that of other churches in that state. Baptists moved into Rhode Island and Pennsylvania was settled by the Quakers.

By the time of the American Revolution the Church of England was represented throughout the colonies. Its growth was the result of two missionary societies formed by Thomas Bray. These societies, still active in the church, are the Society for Promoting Christian Knowledge and the Society for the Propagation of the Gospel.

Unlike other denominations, the Church of England in America (which was later to be called the Episcopal Church) was not an independent church. Although many American Anglicans shared the sympathies of other Americans in regard to independence, as far as their church was concerned they were dependent upon English bishops for the ordination of their clergy. One desiring ordination had to undertake a perilous journey to England. The Bishop of London, three thousand miles away, was in charge of the fortunes of the American church.

The basic reason that the Episcopal Church in the colonies existed without bishops for some 150 years was primarily political. Many colonists saw in the office of bishop a symbol of tyranny. The Whigs in Parliament were neither deaf nor blind to the feelings of their American counterparts. On the other hand, many of the Tories couldn't see any step which might lead to independence from English ecclesiastical control.

At the time of the American Revolution most of the Anglican clergy in America were loyal to England. There were some notable exceptions. Dr. William White of Christ Church, Philadelphia, became chaplain both to the Continental Congress and to the Continental Army. Although the majority of the signers of the Declaration of Independence were Anglicans, the Anglican Church was regarded by many with distrust.

Following the war, the Anglican Church in the colonies faced dark times. The states in the southern colonies, where the Anglican Church had been firmly established, deprived the church of many of its sources of revenue. England withdrew funds and clergy fled to Canada and the West Indies.

However, even in the midst of these problems, Anglicans in the colonies demonstrated a determination to solve their problems, the basic one being the lack of a bishop. Those sects in America which were not dependent upon bishops for confirmation and ordination were making rapid headway in their missionary efforts because they were not bound to any "mother church."

The initiative came from Dr. William White of Philadelphia. In 1783 a convention of clergy met at Woodbury, Connecticut and Dr. Samuel Seabury was elected bishop and sent to England for consecration. Upon his arrival, Seabury's request was refused because English law prevented the consecration or ordination of a clergyman who would not take a loyalty oath to the crown. His next move was to seek ordination at the hands of Scottish bishops, called "non-jurors" because they had remained loyal to the House of Stuart, refusing to recognize the House of Hanover. The Scottish church was not bound by English ecclesiastical law, and these bishops consented to consecrate Dr. Seabury on November 14, 1784.

In 1787, English law having been changed, Dr. Samuel Provoost, rector of Trinity Church, New York City, along with Dr. White, went to England where they were consecrated bishops by the archbishops of Canterbury and York and the bishop of Bath and Wells. Thus our bishops represent both Scottish and English lines of succession.

At Philadelphia, in 1787, a general convention was held at which the church adopted a constitution. The Prayer Book of the English Church was revised for American usage. It was decided to call the church "The Protestant Episcopal Church in the United States." The term *protestant* here was not intended to mean that Episcopalians in America considered themselves Protestants in the same sense as did Lutherans and Presbyterians, but rather in opposition to papal Catholicism.

This convention signaled an opportunity for growth, but growth was slow. Not only had the church lost time because of problems in securing bishops, but the nature of the Episcopal Church with its Prayer Book worship was not appreciated apart from communities of English settlers. It has been said that the Baptists went with their people on foot, the Presbyterians waited for schools, and Episcopalians waited for the Pullman car!

But this was not quite the case. Bishop Hobart in New York and Bishop Griswold in New England awakened the church to mission. In 1819 Philander Chase became bishop of Ohio, and in 1820 the Domestic and Foreign Missionary Society was organized. In 1835 Jackson Kemper was consecrated bishop of the Northwest and the church moved into California in succeeding years. During this same period the General Seminary in New York City and Virginia Theological Seminary in Alexandria, Virginia, were founded.

If the Episcopal Church was left behind numerically in the missionary enterprise, it excelled in the establishment of educational institutions—King's College (re-named Columbia University after the Revolution), William and Mary College, Hobart, Kenyon, the University of the South, and Trinity College. The Episcopal Church has also been prominent in the establishment of preparatory schools. Some of the most noted are Groton, St. Mark's, St. George's, and St. Paul's. Also, seminaries have been established thoughout the United States, Liberia, Haiti, Brazil, and the Philippines.

* * * * *

While Episcopalians have traditionally differed drastically in regard to religious, political, and social issues, and while we continue to differ in regard to the sanctioning of strategies related to ministry in those areas, we are bound together as Anglicans by our commitment to the doctrine of the Incarnation. We believe that God claims all areas of our life as religious. Just as God created people to "have dominion" over the earth by being responsible stewards of its resources, so his sending of Jesus Christ represents his love for the world, his caring for the whole of life. By assuming human form, God entered into history and claims all areas of our life as potentially sacred.

Our church in convention cannot speak for all of us. We have no pope who by unilateral fiat can resolve our arguments over changes in the liturgy or resolve a debate over doctrine. Bishops, priests, and laity are often divided over issues involving the church and social issues. We frequently experience clashes of conscience. Episcopalians, reflecting something of their American heritage, are quick to resist what they perceive to be authoritarian pronouncements by their clergy and, by the same token, the clergy do not yield readily to pressures from laity if those pressures are perceived to be means of silencing the prophetic voice.

We believe that God can and does speak to us through dissent and diversity. We believe that what ultimately destroys an institution is not dissent or even conflict, but despair and cynicism which maintain that nothing we say or do has any meaning. Both the liberal and conservative in our church hold the common conviction that, in regard to the issues of faith and life, silence is not necessarily golden.

The Oxford and the Evangelical Movements

Any understanding of the basic character of the Anglican Communion involves an understanding of the Oxford and Evangelical movements, both of which still exert significant influence.

Inevitably in Inquirers' Classes there comes the time when one is asked what is meant by "high" and "low" Episcopal churches. A standard response is that high churches feature bells rung during certain parts of the Eucharist, incense, chanting parts of the service, people crossing themselves, and genuflections (going down on one knee). In the high church tradition the Eucharist has been the principal service. In contrast, low churches feature Morning Prayer as a norm. The priest wears a surplice and stole, rather than Eucharistic vestments, and there seems to be more emphasis on preaching. In general, such churches reflect the absence of Catholic ceremonial.

Such an answer is reasonably accurate, although it must be noted that the outward and visible signs of worship, the wardrobes of worship, do not necessarily reflect the doctrinal and theological convictions of clergy or laity. Catholic ceremonial may be found in churches where clergy and laity are theologically liberal and open to influences which represent a departure from tradition to low churchmen. I know clergy and laity who, while disavowing high church ceremonial, nevertheless are quite insistent on a high doctrine of episcopacy and are loathe to become involved in what seems to them to smack of liturgical experimentation.

Before we examine the Evangelical and Catholic movements, I must caution you that the Evangelical movement is not necessarily characteristic of low church Episcopalianism. There have been and are Anglicans who, while ceremonially protestant or low, are distrustful of Evangelical emphases. There are high churchmen who are deeply involved in the Evangelical movement. The organization, a few years ago, of the Evangelical Catholic Congress is an example of this.

I think it is significant that the Evangelical movement did not arise in reaction to the presence of Catholic influences in the Church of England. John Wesley and other Evangelical clergy of the eighteenth century were deeply influenced by Catholic tradition in the Church of England, although they were not given to Catholic ceremonial. They were particularly influenced by the Catholic emphasis on fasting and the sacraments.

The Evangelical movement arose in protest to a church captured by what has been called "deism." Deism (from the Latin word for God) emphasized a theology centering on natural revelation rather than revealed religion. The concept of miracle contained in biblical religion was a concept deemed to be impossible for the enlightened man of the eighteenth century. Thomas Jefferson, for example, wrote his own revision of the New Testament by deleting all references to miracle, preserving only the ethical teachings of Jesus.

During the eighteenth century the history of religions became a prominent study. Scholars thought that Christianity could be readily explained in naturalistic terms and by comparison to other religions from which it borrowed, or presumably borrowed. *Miracle* was only a word for what would in time yield to man's reason. It was presumed that God created the world as a watchmaker creates a watch, wound it up, and stepped aside to let it run. He no longer interfered. Contemporary studies have discredited many of the too-neat assumptions of eighteenth-century deists.

Bishops, theologians, clergy, and laity came under this influence with the result that preaching came to be characterized by academic and philosophical discourse. Religious ritual, the life of prayer, the importance of sacraments were largely eclipsed by rationalism. Above all, the Evangelical conviction that the Christian was commissioned by baptism and confirmation to make the Gospel known gave way to the premise that Jesus was only one of a company of prophets, certainly not, as the Acts of the Apostles described him, "the only name under heaven whereby we may be saved." Deism permeated a movement which became known as the Latitudinarian movement, which, as the name implies, gave wide latitude to theologies which did not center in the uniqueness of Christianity.

Bishops and clergy, then, tended to live off their endowments rather than their convictions. The Evangelical movement, represented in priests like the Wesleys, had at its heart the primacy of Scripture and the imperative to preach by way of creating conviction and conversion. While many Evangelical clergy and laity remained within the Church of England (without them there would have been no missionary thrust), the Methodist movement, against the wishes of John Wesley, formed another church. All Evangelicals, however, agreed on the necessity of experiencing new life in the Holy Spirit, conversion, and the "new birth."

Turning to the Oxford movement, it is significant that the restoration of Catholic faith and ceremonial did not arise as a protest to the Evangelical movement but, as the Evangelical movement, it found itself in reaction to a Latitudinarian church—a church having become comfortably secular and readily submitting to policies of the state.

In 1833 a group of Oxford scholars and churchmen began to issue tracts and sermons confronting the Church of England with its need to affirm its Catholic heritage, to declare its autonomy over and against the state.

It is noteworthy that John Henry Newman, the leading figure of this movement, was nourished in his youth in the Evangelical tradition. Many of his sermons evidence this heritage. By the middle of the nineteenth century the Evangelical movement had become respectable and established, having lost much of its fervor, indeed having become institutionalized. Newman, Pusey, and other notables believed that the challenge of secularism, the spiritual apathy of the nation, could only be countered by a reaffirmation of the Catholic heritage of the church, a heritage latent and ready for resurrection.

Just as the Evangelical movement produced the Society for the Propagation of the Gospel, so the Oxford movement brought forth the founding of monasteries and the restoration of the Eucharist as the primary act of worship. The Romantic movement in literature and art created a climate in which this movement found expression and hospitality. Although many clergy suffered because of "Romish" tendencies, the Oxford movement captured the imagination of multitudes of churchmen.

Vested choirs, processional crosses, candles on the altar, indeed the restoration of Gothic architecture, represent in part the legacy of the Oxford movement. Life and worship in a contemporary Episcopal church reflect the influences of all of these movements.

The Charismatic Movement

At the international congress of the Catholic Charismatic Renewal, in the presence of 750 concelebrating priests and 10,000 people representing various denominations, Cardinal Suenens offered an extemporaneous prophecy. In all probability it was the first of its kind to be offered at a Mass at St. Peter's, Rome. The following are a few of the statements which Cardinal Suenens believed to be given to him by the Holy Spirit.

> I have strengthened you with my power. I will renew my Church. I will lead my people to a new unity. . . . I am creating for myself anew an army of witnesses and bringing my people together. . . . Allow yourself to be permeated by me. Experience my life, my spirit, my power. . . . I have begun to renew my Church.

The Reverend Robert Hawn, formerly Executive Secretary of the Episcopal Charismatic Fellowship, said recently:

> We have to recognize the outpouring of the Holy Spirit in the world today. The Lord is calling his people together. He wants to restore the Church with the original power and witness which came from the first Pentecost, and so he is calling them together from across denominational boundaries, because the Holy Spirit does not know denominations.

Episcopalians and members of other traditional denominations are being confronted by such phrases as "baptism in the Spirit" and such phenomena as speaking and singing in tongues, the offering of prophecies, the laying on of hands for healing, not just by the clergy, but by laity present. "Eucharists in a Charismatic Mode" are part of the life of St. Philip's Cathedral, Atlanta, the largest Episcopal parish in the United States, as they also have become part of the life of many parishes and small missions throughout Anglicanism.

The Charismatic movement has been greeted by fascination and fear, by rage and rejoicing (as was the Oxford Movement). The seeming betrayal of predictable and orderly worship has angered and confused those who have come to Episcopalianism as refugees from revivalism. On the other hand, an increasing number of Episcopalians have come to discover in charismatic worship not the denial of liturgy, but a free-flowing liturgy, permitting the spontaneous response to the presence of the Holy Spirit. While some Charismatics have left the church to form communities of their own, it is increasingly evident that the Charismatic movement in our church manifests the centrality of the Eucharist and all of the sacraments, along with submission to the authority of the constitution and canons of the church.

Charismatic comes from the Greek word *charisma* or "gift." While Catholic, Orthodox, and Protestant tradition has always affirmed gifts of the Spirit through sacramental systems, as well as personal inspiration by the Holy Spirit, there has been a traditional distrust of the manifestation of such gifts of prophecy, healing, and especially speaking in tongues or glossalalia.

Just as vestments, incense, and chanting represented the outward and visible sign of a Catholic, and just as preaching outside of the church building came to characterize the Evangelical, so in the case of the Charismatic movement, speaking, praying, singing in tongues has come to represent what is certainly the primary issue in charismatic renewal.

Several things need to be said about this phenomenon. First, glossalalia is not unique to Christianity, but was a part of the Hellenistic mystical religions of the ancient world. It is also present in other religions. It has always been present in the spiritual life of Christians through the centuries.

Second, although glossalalia has been reported as the miracle of the speaker speaking a language not known to him (as in Acts 2:6-11), the primary function of this phenomenon lies in the experience of a "prayer language." As St. Paul noted, "...one who speaks in a tongue speaks not to men but to God; for . . . he utters mysteries in the Spirit" (I Corinthians 14:2). Prayer in tongues represents a surrender of the tongue to God. Our Lord defined God as "Spirit," saying "and those who worship him must worship in spirit and in truth" (John 4:24). Our spirit in submission to a God who cannot be expressed totally in rational language can involve this experience. A father or mother often speak in nonsense language to their infant, but the language conveys the communion of love and profound adoration.

Third, a careful reading of I Corinthians 12-14 reveals that, although St. Paul said "I thank God that I speak in tongues more than you all," this gift of the Spirit is ranked last in the list of ministries given in I Corinthians 12:27ff. because it had assumed an importance out of proportion to its purpose and had become a sign of spiritual elitism.

It is important to say something about prophecy here for, although St. Paul said "I want you all to speak in tongues," he went on to say "but even more to prophesy" (I Corinthians 14:5). Interestingly enough, after the ministry of the apostles, which he ranks first (I Corinthians 12:28), the role of prophecy is mentioned. "...He who prophesies speaks to men for their upbuilding and encouragement and consolation" (I Corinthians 14:3). True prophecy according to II Peter 1:21 is not "by the impulse of man, but men moved by the Holy Spirit."

The Charismatic movement recognizes that prophecy may come from those who are not clergy. I have experienced on numerous occasions the offering of a verse of Scripture or an utterance in the first person which serves to clarify an issue or console someone present. The prophecy given by Cardinal Suenens is an example of what can happen in a small gathering. True prophecy is consistent with Scripture and tradition. This is why it is important that the authority of the church be represented by the presence of clergy or laity who know the Scriptures and are competent theologians, appreciative of the sacramental nature of the church. St. Paul says, "I will pray with the Spirit and I will pray with the mind also. . ." (I Corinthians 14:15). Mindless emotionalism and hysteria are revelations not of the Spirit of God but of the spirit of confusion.

This brings us to two significant criticisms of the Charismatic movement, one of which comes from secular sources and the other from religious sources.

The first criticism accuses the Charismatic movement of being simply a response to an age of technology, an age which makes us feel victimized by abstract forces over which we have no control and by an anonymous, bureaucratic big government. In our reaction against scientific rationalism, we turn to psychologies involving group encounter or to religious experiences which promise ecstasy, deliverance, and a new status through "baptism in the Spirit."

Through the ages movements of renewal and restoration have in large measure been reactions against prevailing cultural trends. But why shouldn't they be? The church is under no obligation to be passive in regard to the prevailing culture. Monasticism, the Evangelical and the Oxford movements illustrate renewal which does not seek escape from the world, but rather opportunities for equipping spiritually those who are called to live in the world. "Renewal," "life in the Spirit," "baptism in the Spirit," by whatever name we describe it, charismatic experience has been the experience of many in the scientific, business, and academic communities, and it has been an experience renewing the whole person in understanding the world, indeed overcoming the world. It is not necessarily spiritual obscurantism.

The religious objection, voiced mainly by conservative Protestant sources, sees the Charismatic movement as an impossibility because, they say, the charismatic manifestations of the Spirit were given only to the apostolic church for the purpose of creating faith until the Scriptures could finally be compiled. This is called dispensationalism. God granted a particular dispensation of the Spirit and later withdrew it.

Another objection, closely akin to this one, is heard from Catholic and Orthodox sources. They say that charismatic ministries shared in the primitive church by the laity are now represented solely by the clergy. Ernst Troeltsch, one of the great historians of the church, calls this "the routinization of charisma." By this he means that charisma-spiritual gifts became the property of the clergy to dispense through the sacraments because of the need for priestly authority over the ecstatic and often irresponsible behavior of the laity.

The problem with dispensationalism is that it seems to assign the empowering presence of the Holy Spirit only to that church described on the day of Pentecost in the second chapter of the Acts of the Apostles. The problem with this view, say some traditionalists, is that it assumes the incompatibility of clergy and laity ministering in concert and that God's spiritual gifts are necessarily the property of the ordained clergy. This overlooks the quite orthodox belief that the Holy Spirit is given in baptism and confirmation and manifestations of that Spirit may well be displayed in ministries of the laity. During visitations to charismatic parishes I have noticed obedience to the clergy who, in turn by the authority vested in them as priests, are enabling laity to discover their spiritual ministries.

A final observation: The Charismatic movement is no exception to the tendency that movements of restoration and renewal have toward becoming elitist. "I am more Catholic than thou." "I am more Protestant than thou." "I am more spiritual than thou." "I am more reasonably religious than thou."

The key phrase of the Charismatic movement is "baptism in the Spirit." It is a Scriptural phrase, but it refers to all of us who have been baptized in water and been confirmed, for the Holy Spirit is given at these events, just as the Spirit is invoked at the altar to transform the bread and wine into the body and blood of Christ. God has gifted us in his sacraments. All of us are implicity Charismatics.

The scenario of salvation cannot be totally systematized into any one scheme. If the Spirit is imparted through the sacraments, it also comes to us through prayer and the reading of Scripture. The Spirit is not an abstract force but the very person of God. The Spirit is received through the laying on of hands (Acts 8:11). The Spirit is bestowed following water baptism (Acts 2:38). The Spirit precedes baptism in water (Acts 10:44).

"Having gifts that differ according to the grace given to us," said St. Paul, "let us use them" (Romans 12:6). God has gifted us with a church at once Catholic, Evangelical, and Charismatic, a church whose mission it is to renew itself even as it proclaims the gospel to the world.

V. The Bible

In my first mission church, an elderly woman visited us frequently. She was a Primitive Baptist. When I asked her how it was that a Primitive Baptist found happiness in our church, she explained that she loved to visit us because we read more from the Bible than her church did. It is immediately evident to the visitor of an Episcopal church that the reading of Scripture is primary to the experience of worship. Indeed, nearly four-fifths of the Prayer Book is derived from Scripture.

What Is the Bible?

The word *Bible* comes from a Greek word *biblos,* meaning papyrus—the reed used in the making the "paper" upon which early Scriptures were written. In time papyrus was replaced by vellum (parchment) and the codex or book form. The Bible is both a collection of books—a library—and a single book; but it is a book that varied in its contents until the middle of the fourth century.

The Bible is valued for a variety of reasons. There are whose who value it as a monument to classical Hebrew, and *Koine* Greek—the common Greek of the day. There are those who value the Bible as indispensable to the study of the ancient empires of the Middle East. To others the Bible represents a treasury of ethical wisdom and practical precepts for the virtuous life. Many who hold these views tend either to discount or to deny the problematic presence of the supernatural and the presence of myth.

Because the presence of myth in the Scriptures has, for many, mitigated against any meaning the Scriptures might have other than their value as literature, wisdom, and history, I think it is important that we explore the meaning of the word *myth.* In popular understanding a myth tends to appear as a word for something that is not true.

However, a myth is another word for a story, a story which may be true or false. A myth is a story which attempts to describe abstract or eternal truths in concrete, pictorial words. The difference between myth in the Judeo-Christian faith and other religions is that in our faith myth has as its reference a God who acts in history, who initiates an encounter with his creatures. Myth can be cleverly devised as was the Nazis' myth of the "master race," drawn from pagan mythology. Communism's vision of the classless society is a vision dramatized by rituals setting forth mythical pictures in which this secular faith will capture ultimately the imagination and loyalty of all people.

But myth in the Bible, unlike the myths of Gnosticism, does not represent the imaginative speculation of man with his visions and fantasies, but rather myth is occasioned by the experiences of those who were "eyewitnesses" of God's activity in history. The most casual reading of Scripture reveals a God who encounters, confronts, demands, and invites a response from man. God is not another name for the object of ethical and philosophical speculation. While myths are incapable of certain kinds of factual verification, as are tape recordings of an event, myths are not simply tales.

To be true, a myth must resonate to the realities of human experience—our hope, our human nature, what it feels like to be alienated, to experience the presence of death, to know joy, peace, and forgiveness. A man in my parish who has begun to read the Bible seriously said to a study group, "I am finally finding out who I am." To which I might say, "and also to whom you belong and God's purpose for you."

The Bible continues to be a bestseller not because it is unbelievable, but because it is believable. Someone has said, "It is not the things in the Bible which I don't understand that bother me, but the things I do understand." When Peter said to Jesus, "Lord, to whom shall we go? You have the words of eternal life. . ." (John 6:68ff.), he foreshadowed the reason for Article VI of our Articles of Religion—"Of the Sufficiency of the Holy Scriptures for Salvation."

The Word of God or the Word of Man

For many, the Bible represents either the word of God or the word of man. That is, either the Bible is divinely inspired, hence not open to critical study, or else it is only a human composition, an anthology of human inspiration.

Both of these perspectives are not without some truth. The Bible is more than the inspirational literary efforts of man. Man's words in

Scripture represent his attempt to set forth the Word God has spoken. Man can speak of God only because God has spoken first. On the other hand, the imagination of man, his creative and critical faculties, are vehicles of his response to God.

Some who view the Bible as divinely inspired tend to assume that the Bible is off limits to historical, literary, and linguistic criticism which are legitimate in the study of other kinds of literature. Indeed the word *criticism* is often perceived as meaning to tear down, hence to be negative. But criticism can have a positive function. Indeed, as I noted earlier, the collection of Scripture representing our authorized canon was derived both by the inspiration of the Holy Spirit, and the critical faculties of the early Christians who had to separate the real from the spurious, the Gnostic gospels.

Certainly, critical efforts can tend to fragment the Scriptures to such an extent that we see the trees rather than the forest, a collection of fascinating bits of archaic information and interesting literary forms, rather than the drama of salvation. On the other hand, the alternative of what has been called "verbal inspiration" unfortunately assumes that the writers of Scripture were reduced to automatons by the Holy Spirit. Every noun, adjective, verb, and preposition was given to them.

The human spirit participated in the revelations of the divine Spirit. Certainly, no great expression of creativity can be *only* human. After all of the critical tools have been applied to any enduring expression of art, there remains the presence of creativity in touch with reality beyond itself. I know a young poet who writes excellent poetry but claims no belief in God, except that occasionally he uses the words *inspired* or *moved* to account for something he has written. The Bible is the result of an interplay between the Spirit of God moving upon the restless, yearning, and creative spirit of his creatures.

Divine Inspiration

Anglicans appreciate this interplay, representing the attempt of biblical man to discover the words expressive of God's revelation. The Bible is indeed the word of God. The Bible is true, but its truth is not a matter of its being in accord with contemporary hypotheses of science, nor is its truth, as the saving knowledge of God, affected by variations in the transmissions of the various texts.

In the last century there was an enormous controversy over Darwin's theory of evolution; it still rages in parts of the United States. The Scopes' trial dramatized an issue that had been around for some time. What seemed to be at stake was the entire credibility of the Bible: If the biblical account of creation wasn't true, what in the Bible was?

Darwin's theory of evolution has, of course, given way to other speculations on the origin of creation. For example, the works of Loren Eisley and the books of the Jesuit theologian and paleontologist Pierre Teilhard de Chardin represent understandings of the evolutionary process at odds with earlier theories of evolution.

In our discussion of some of the ways the presence of Christ was explained at the Eucharist, we noted that these explanations were representations of the ages in which they emerged. They served as vehicles for getting at what is essentially mystery. Thus, while we deny as Christians the explanation of the universe as an accidental "big bang," we do affirm creation as the work of God. We affirm a creation through which the Holy Spirit is still at work, enabling us to understand it and appropriate its mysteries.

The Bible is not antiscientific but prescientific. The cosmology of the ancient Hebrew is not ours, but his belief in purposive creation is, and even in his view there is variation. In chapter one of Genesis, God calls all things into existence ("Let there be. . ."). In the second chapter God is described as walking in the garden, molding man from the earth. In one view, God is transcendent to creation, in the other view he is immanent, he comes into the garden. Both views are true about God. We are reasonably certain that chapter one of Genesis was written by a priest in the fifth century B.C. during the time of the Second Temple. What was important to him was that the sequence of God's creative activity ended in the institution of the Sabbath rather than in the culmination of creation in man.

Chapter two reflects a more human understanding of God, who personally confronts his rebellious creatures rather than dealing with them by fiat from afar. Many of the most dramatic and intensely personal stories of the Old Testament had their origin in traditions known to this storyteller, for he was no priest or theologian.

We also notice in the Hebrew text different names for God—the word *elohim* and the word *yahweh*. The former is plural in form; the latter is derived from the Hebrew verb "to be" and probably means something like, "He who calls all things into existence, or causes to be." This name was given by a particular revelation to Moses, not to be uttered because it was the intimate name of God, reflective of the understanding of ancient man (and primitives today) that to know a person's name is to have authority over that person.

Hebrew was written without vowels until some centuries after the time of Christ when scribes entered vowel signs into the text. What they did was to substitute the word *Lord* or *adonai,* or rather its vowels, for the word *yahweh,* hence leading later translators to translate the word as Jehovah. But the sacred name, the four consonants YHWH stood in the text as the most sacred revelation.

We note the presence of anachronisms in Scripture. An anachronism is the use of something not consistent with the time in which it was used. For example, Shakespeare mentions in some of his plays the use of gunpowder, at a time it was unknown. Camels mentioned in Genesis indicate the presence of an animal unknown at that early period. It is highly improbable that Moses wrote all of the first five books of the Bible (one of the assumptions held by those who believe divine inspiration requires this). For one thing, it is unlikely that he could have written about his own death (Deuteronomy 34:1-8)!

A careful reading of the Bible indicates more than one account of the same episode. One account of the anointing of Saul as king by the prophet Samuel states that this action was a directive of God. Another source describes Samuel as reluctantly submitting to the cries of the people that he be king. There are two accounts of how Beersheba got its name (Genesis 21:31, 26:33), two accounts of the banishment of Hagar and Ishmael (Genesis 16:6-16, 21:9-21). Other examples could be cited.

There are aspects of legislation and cultic acts which do not mean the same to us today as they did to biblical man. Do we believe that God tried to kill Moses but relented because Moses performed an act of circumcision? Certainly the leprosy laws of Leviticus are of no value to us, nor do we regard it as inspired revelation (from God) to kill the inhabitants of a captured city.

My older brother, an English professor, told me about one of his students who insisted upon the literal meaning of Scripture. When he asked her about the meaning of the Song of Solomon (the most highly erotic book in the Bible) she instantly replied, "But that is an allegory about Christ and his church."

Whatever our view of Scripture, especially in reference to verbal inspiration, there will always be some things that are more meaningful to us than others. Just as we are told in St. Luke's Gospel that Jesus "grew in wisdom and in stature," so also, from the time of the patriarchs to his coming, the community of faith grew in its appropriation of God's revelation.

While biblical theology tells us of God, it most certainly reveals a lot about ourselves, our prejudices and perspectives. Since the beginning of this century, archeology has confirmed much of the accuracy of the

Bible's reporting of historical events. The assumption that the Bible could be only understood and explained by reference to phenomena in other religions has largely been abandoned. Hebrew worship and life is unique in many ways and it reflects more than one way of understanding the will of God. For example, although the Hebrews worshiped one God, they disagreed about the place of worship. The Samaritans on the basis of Scripture and tradition believed Mt. Gerizim to be the authorized place of worship; the Jews opted for Jerusalem. Some Jews were opposed to kingship, preferring the days of the tribal confederacy. Just as in our folklore stories about an actual event in history may vary, so also did theirs. The diversity of perspective in the Scriptures attests to the reality of historical happenings and presents to us a people eminently believable.

The meaning of God's revelation cannot be exhaustively captured by any one perspective (note four accounts of the resurrection). But the meaning of revelation is not invalidated by a frequently heard assumption that the recording of events in Scripture is too far removed from the events themselves, with the added assertion that variants in the texts refute the certainty of divine revelation.

While many have unquestionably assumed the essential reliability of other texts of classical antiquity, F. G. Kenyon notes that, for example, the earliest manuscript of Virgil that we now possess was copied some 350 years after his death. For all other classical writers, the interval between the date of the author and the earliest extant manuscript of his works is much greater."[1] We have discovered papyri of the New Testament which bring us to within 120 years of the ministry of Jesus. The discovery of the Dead Sea Scrolls in 1947 reveals a painstakingly accurate copying of Scripture, indicating little variation, as compared to succeeding texts.

William Barclay says that, although there are 150,000 places in which we have variant readings in the texts, "fewer than 400 affect the sense, fewer than 50 are of any importance, and there is no case in which an article of faith or a precept of duty is left in doubt."[2]

Thus the Bible does not need for its divine inspiration the painstaking efforts of scholars to explain away all variations and discrepancies to preserve literal truth or verbal inspiration. Nor do we need to take seriously accusations implying its basic inaccuracy, for the Bible not only has a way of surviving its critics but converting some of them!

The Word of God

I have tried to clarify the distinction between belief in the Bible as divinely inspired and the doctrine of verbal infallibility or inerrancy.

There is a saying to the effect that "the Bible is not the word of God; it contains the Word of God." The Bible as the Word of God leads to the creation of a "paper pope." A multitude of denominations has been the result of appeals to Scripture.

The Bible affords a happy hunting ground of proof texts for those seeking justification for what it is that seems important to them. None of us approaches the reading and study of Scripture without bringing something to our encounter. Our prejudices can usually be confirmed by some particular passage. Just about any point can be proved.

I recall an angry woman who said she wanted the Lord's Prayer "just the way Jesus said it" (referring to the King James translation). But a precise translation of the Aramaic in which he spoke is impossible.

In a similar example, the Lord's Prayer in Matthew's Gospel differs from Luke's account, for Matthew adds the doxology, "For thine is the kingdom, the power, and the glory." The early church added this doxology because it gave the prayer a liturgical flow.

A final example can be found in Mark 10:2-9; Jesus gives no grounds for divorce, but in Matthew 5:31 adultery is given as a permissible ground. Some churches have followed Mark and others Matthew. Certainly one can say that Jesus changed his mind, or that one of them is the true saying, but for verbal inerrancy this raises a problem. The Anglican response to this kind of dilemma is to say that some of the sayings of Jesus were remembered differently and, through the continual guidance of the Holy Spirit, his teachings were applied. The Scriptures are the library of the church, describing the way Jesus and his teachings were remembered.

But as I noted earlier, diversity of perspective in the transmission of testimony need not annul the truth behind the testimony. Any comparison of the teachings and movements of Jesus described in the Gospels reflect considerable variation. For example, the cleansing of the Temple appears early in John's Gospel but in the other three it comes at the end of his ministry. The Evangelists had a purpose in the way they arranged their Gospels.

It is through study, prayer, and the hearing of preaching that Scripture "speaks" to us. Its truths are not just a matter of personal or private interpretation. We often use the expression "to leave word" in regard to a message. Unless we are involved in the C.I.A. or in a situation where the words represent a precise code, it is not important if our exact words are used. It is the message we intend to convey.

Thus we might say that the Bible is a library of messages, God's communication to us. Many of these messages in the Bible come to us in the experiences of biblical man and woman. God speaks through events and, as these experiences become ours, we encounter the living God. For example, we may experience communion with God as we hear another person describe an experience which has brought either hope or despair. When the preacher proclaims the Word of God, that message comes to us through the presence of the preacher. It is not just a matter of his reading Scripture, but the revelation comes through his words, indeed through what he or she says nonverbally.

Certainly, this raises the question of how, given the varying interpretations of Scripture by theologians, clergy, and sincere laity, we can discern what is of God and what is of men. I can respond only in a personal way. In preparing a teaching or a sermon, after I read the biblical texts, I spend time in prayer and reflection and think about other tasks in my ministry. Then I compare commentaries which may lead to new insights or the revision and implementation of my own encounter with the texts. I seek to discern as much as possible the mind of the church. Rarely is the sermon given in total accord with the prepared manuscript; but in the encounter with the congregation—that process not only of my speaking to them, but in a kind of dialogue and conversation with them—the sermon is often revised in the process of being delivered.

Certainly I can get in the way of the message that God would communicate through me. My emotional state, the wrong choice of words, attempts to be clever or intellectual can subvert what it is God wishes to speak through me. But also it is true that the spiritual, psychological, and emotional state of the hearer can affect what is heard. I pray before the altar immediately prior to my sermon and I think it is important that the congregation pray for me so that God can come between us.

This process is not without application to the lay person to whom there are available excellent and readable resources for Bible study. The Bible is a book to be read not alone, but in community. Its truths are truths we hold in community, together, as the body of Christ, his church. It is the presence of the Holy Spirit which verifies to us the power, joy, and peace that is God's Word to us. God's messages come through us and to us often not because of ourselves, but in spite of ourselves.

Jesus Christ as the Word

It is unfortunate that arguments over the inerrancy of Scripture, both by those who defend verbal inspiration and those who are totally agnostic in regard to the meaning and value of its words, tend to identify the words of the text with the Word of God. Thus the texts themselves come to represent the revelation. If asked "What is the word of God?" the average layman most probably would say "the Bible."

Such an answer does not sufficiently take into account the truth that, for Christians, the Word of God is Jesus Christ. In a real although mysterious sense, Jesus Christ is God's speech to us. "He who has seen me has seen the Father," he said to his disciples. Hymn 402 of the Episcopal Hymnal says of the Bible, "It is the heaven-drawn picture of Christ, the living Word."

In the twenty-fourth chapter of St. Luke's Gospel, Jesus appears as a stranger to two men walking to the village of Emmaus. They are disheartened and defeated in the wake of the crucifixion. Jesus approaches them and says as they walk along together, "Was it not necessary that Christ should suffer these things and enter into his glory?" Then Luke records, "And beginning with Moses and all the prophets, he interpreted to them in all the scriptures the things concerning himself" (Luke 24:27).

While there are various perspectives which are valid in the approach to Scripture and varying ways in which we perceive the value of Scripture, the Christian church has seen in the Scriptures the unfolding drama of God and a people which required or made necessary the sacrifice and resurrection of Christ.

In the Old Testament God revealed himself as creator and lawgiver, through whose Spirit the prophets were raised up. The Law, as we noted earlier, served as a means to keep the community together, to give it identity in the midst of pagan nations.

However, law does not interpret itself any more than Scripture interprets itself. Law needs the interpretation of courts, commentaries, and jurists. But more than these, law needs the prophet to point to its true purpose, to its fulfillment. In every age law has been used to protect special interests, to exclude rather than to include. In the Old Testament prophets were raised up by the Spirit of God. It was their calling to tell forth the moral and spiritual implications of the Law.

Jesus sadly noted that his people tended to ignore and kill the prophets. The people of Israel possessed a rich deposit of Law, with commentary and interpretation. They came to possess a great heritage of prophecy. But in spite of it all, many of them were far from experiencing the Kingdom of God to which it all pointed and for which it was designed. Simply put, the meaning of God's incarnation as man was to personalize the words, directives, legislation, and prophecies of the past.

Some say that a person "is as good as his word," which means that he is what he says he is, that there is a correlation between his words and his actions. Few conversions occur because of the testimony and argumentation of words. It is the life behind the words which is or is not convincing and the life or the person is the word.

The Christian community experienced in Jesus Christ the presence of Law, but Law that was personal, manifest not only in judgment but in healing and restoration. In him they saw prophecy, not merely of the future, but of the present, the Kingdom in their midst. God's Spirit which moved at creation had become enfleshed. Thus when we speak of Jesus Christ as the Word of God we are not simply speaking of his teachings (which bear similarity to some of the teachings of the prophets and other rabbis), but we are speaking of the person that is Jesus the Christ. Hence, for the early Christians the messenger was greater than his message, the teacher was greater than his teaching. In word and deed Jesus Christ was God's speech to us, his conversation with us.

In the third chapter of the Acts of the Apostles, Peter speaks of Jesus as the "Author of life" (Acts 3:15). The word carries with it the notion of creativity. Indeed he has the "words of life" because he *is* the Word of life seeking expression in the words of men.

The Canon of the Old Testament

The word *canon* is derived from a Greek word meaning "measure" or "rule." When used in regard to the Bible, this term refers to the authoritative standard or collection of books by which others are judged. The process of canonization refers to the way some books, rather than others, were given authority. The Old Testament and the New Testament canons we have today are but portions of the literature of the Jewish and Christian people. For example, references are made in Joshua to the Book of Jashar (Joshua 10:13), and in Numbers there is a reference to the Book of the Wars of the Lord (Numbers 21:14), books no longer extant.

The first move toward canonization came in 621 B.C. when what we know as the book of Deuteronomy was discovered, hidden in the Temple during the reign of King Josiah. He declared it to state authoritatively both the proper way to worship and the proper meaning of present legislation.

During the period following the exile, the period which saw the rebuilding of the Temple, the Jews became, in the fullest sense, "the people of the Book." The scribes of that time were obsessed by a desire to preserve their heritage. The books of Ezra and Nehemiah reflect their concern with racial purity and the proper procedures for worship. During this period it was believed that all prophecy had ceased. God's law had been given to Moses; revelation had ended. Now it was a matter of defining and preserving the faith.

The process of canonization was accelerated by two factors. First, during the period following the exile in the sixth century B.C., there arose a type of literature known as *apocalyptic,* from the Greek word for "disclosure" or "revelation." Apocalyptic literature is expressed in highly visionary terms, featuring fanciful images and symbols.

Another characteristic of this kind of literature is its anonymity. The writer ascribed his book to a figure from the past—Abraham, Enoch, or Moses—to insure its acceptance and hence its survival. Most apocalyptic books were evidently the work of contemporary writers who attached the name of a canonized author.

Second, the process of canonization was furthered by the rise of the Christian movement and its ever-increasing literature, already beginning to be considered Scripture. Much of Scripture literature, bordering as it did on the apocalyptic, claimed to be the key unlocking the true meaning of the Old Testament. In Jamnia in 90 A.D. a council of rabbis gathered to close the canon of the Old Testament to further writings and presumed revelations.

The Old Testament canon represents three sections: the Law, comprising the first five books of the Bible (allegedly written by Moses); the Prophets; and the Writings (books like Proverbs and the Psalms). The law was codified during the time of Ezra and Nehemiah (around 500 B.C.), the Prophets were canonized around 250 B.C., and the Writings were given their definitive collection at Jamnia.

The Apocrypha

In the lectionary of the Prayer Book certain books are italicized. These are found in the Apocrypha, a term similar in meaning to apocalypse—"the hidden things." We often use this word to describe an improbable story. In a strict sense, however, we cannot say that the apocryphal writings are false, but with Protestants and Anglicans they have not carried the same weight as they have with Roman Catholics.

The Anglican Communion regards the Apocrypha as providing, in the words of Article VI, "example of life and instruction of manners";

but unlike the Roman Catholic Church, we do not regard the Apocrypha as providing sources of doctrine.

The writings known as apocryphal emerged during the period of Persian and Greek domination of the Jews. Numbering some fifteen books, they afford examples of courage and patriotism. The story of *Bel and the Dragon* (used as a model for detective stories by Dorothy Sayers) and the book of *Judith* are masterpieces of suspense.

In the third century B.C., Jews living in Egypt wanted their own translation of the Bible into Greek, which they spoke. Many of these Jews had never been to Palestine and did not know Hebrew. A translation was issued and tradition has it that there were seventy translators. Hence this edition is known as the Septuagint, designated by the Latin numeral LXX. In the Septuagint, the Apocrypha was included along with other books, but the Hebrew canon of Palestinian Judaism placed the Apocrypha outside of the canon. The early Christians, although using the Septuagint as their reference, did not quote from the Apocrypha, tending to agree with the Palestinian Hebrew version in matters of revelation and faith. The variations in the canon of the Hebrew, Septuagint, Latin, and English versions invite fascinating study, again testifying to the diversity of opinion.

The Canon of the New Testament

The early Christians relied heavily on the Old Testament for "proof texts" of the ministry and passion of Jesus. In time there appeared a collection of his sayings which scholars have come to call the "Q" source. This collection has disappeared except for what we find in the Gospels. The epistles of St. Paul preceded the writing of the Gospels. St. Mark's Gospel appeared about 60 A.D. in Rome, and traditional scholarship believes it to be the first one.

Matthew and Luke relied upon this chronology, but each of them had access to material unknown to the other. For instance, the parable of the Good Samaritan is found in Luke but not in the other Gospels. Matthew, Mark, and Luke represent what we call the Synoptic Gospels, which means they can be compared in terms of basic similarities. The Gospel of St. John, believed to be the last to appear (90–100 A.D.), differs radically in its chronology and vocabulary, a highly literate form of Greek.

The Gospels were not intended to be biographies. They were written to set forth the church's experience and memory of Jesus. In a sense, the Gospels are impressionistic portraits representing various angles of vision. They were written backwards. The event of the resurrection both confirmed and created the faith that Jesus was more than a human teacher. Thus the resurrection narratives came first. The parables and other teachings came next, and finally the birth narratives, which appear only in Matthew and Luke.

As I noted earlier in my discussion of Gnosticism, other Gospels competed for inclusion in the canon. Many of these Gospels heaped miracle upon miracle to the point of overkill. In one of them Jesus is making clay birds as a child and bringing them to life. In another he is presented watching his own death from the Mount of Olives.

Marcion, a famous Gnostic, was instrumental in accelerating the church's movement toward establishing a canon. On the basis of his belief that the God of the Old Testament was the creator of matter and hence evil, and because of his assumption that Law in the Old Testament represented the evil of legalism, he provided for his followers a canon which included every kind of nonlegalistic writing. St. Paul was of primary importance to Marcion because of St. Paul's seeming reaction to the inferior revelation of God in the past.

Toward the end of the second century a man by the name of Montanus appeared proclaiming that he was the promised Spirit and the end of the world was at hand. Thus, as was the case with Judaism, the church was confronted with the imperative to bring its canon to a close, to set forth the genuine over against the spurious.

About 170 A.D. a list of New Testament writings appeared which scholars call the Muratorian Canon. It contained most of what we now know as the New Testament. Apostolic authorship was verified and early bishops such as Ignatius, Polycarp, and Iraneus referred in their letters to all of the twenty-seven books which now comprise our New Testament canon. Thus, both the emergence of the apostolic ministry and the setting forth of the church's canon of Scripture represented ways of dealing with individual attempts to provide doctrine and Scripture.

When Constantine was emperor, he asked Eusebius, bishop of Caesarea, to prepare fifty copies of those Scriptures held in greatest regard by the church. This task was completed in 323 A.D. It was not until some seventy-five years later that the great John Chrysostom used the term *biblia* to refer to this collection. In 397 A.D. at the Council of Carthage the Old and New Testaments were formally canonized by the church.

Which Bible Shall I Read?

A variety of revisions are available. The King James Version is un-excelled in literary quality. It was a Puritan, John Reynolds, who prompted James I to initiate a translation of the Scriptures. This task was carried out mainly by Anglican scholars who, with their Puritan counterparts, wrote in the preface, "We have on the one side avoided the scrupulosities of the Puritans, who leave the olde Ecclesiastical words . . . as also on the other side we have shunned the obscurities of the Papists. . . ."

The translators of the King James Version, however, did not have the Codex Vaticanus and the Codex Sinaiticus, two manuscripts which became available to translators in the nineteenth century. The Revised Standard Version (the New Testament was published in 1946 and the Old Testament in 1952) built upon preceding versions. It reflects the discovery of early papyri and particularly the Isaiah text of the Dead Sea Scrolls.

The New English Bible, completed in 1970, represents an attempt, as it says, "to render the Greek, as we understand it, into the English of the present day . . . to avoid archaism, jargon, and all that is either stilted or slipshod. . . ." J. B. Phillips, in his *Letters to Young Churches* and his translation of the Gospels, preceded the purpose of the translators of the New English Bible. Phillips' translations are excellent.

The Good News Bible has superceded in popularity the New English Bible. This translation is intended for people everywhere for whom English is either their mother tongue or an acquired language. It is a translation into "common" English. Similar in popularity is the Living Bible, which is not a translation but a paraphrase. Its author, Kenneth Taylor, said that he attempted to provide "a restatement of an author's thoughts, using different words than he did."

The popular New American Standard Bible represents the work of Evangelical scholars and adheres closely to the literal text, while employing a kind of King James style. The Jerusalem Bible is a very accurate translation which tends, however, to be pedestrian at times. Its significance lies in the fact that it represents the collective efforts of Protestant, Catholic, and Jewish translators.

I commend the study edition of this translation, along with the New Oxford Annotated Bible (RSV) as excellent resources for Bible study. In every age we confront the imperative of translating the Word of God into the language of our time, in the light of ancient manuscripts which may be discovered. A visitor to a church I once served asked why we did not have an open Bible in the center of our altar. I acknowledged the good intent behind that custom, dramatizing as it does the primacy of Scripture. But I told her the reason we don't place the Bible in the center of the altar is that we do not worship the Scriptures but the Author of Scripture. The Bible is to be read, and that is why it is on the lectern.

In the drama of which God is the author, set forth in the Scriptures, we see our own drama and story, the interplay of the human spirit and the Holy Spirit.

VI. "Why Creeds?"

Christians who claim, "We have no creed but the Bible," are reflecting an impatience, if not a hostility, toward creeds. They are saying that creeds by and large have succeeded only in adding to and perhaps muddying up the clear revelation of Scripture.

Yet all of us live by some kind of creed; the word itself, derived from *credo,* simply means "I believe." Our Bill of Rights and the Declaration of Independence are creeds of a sort. The *Communist Manifesto* is a creed. A creed may not be formally articulated yet still be a set of assumptions by which we live.

The earliest creed in the New Testament might be summed up as "Jesus is Lord." The basic question asked at confirmation is "Will you follow Jesus Christ as your Lord and Savior?" The Christian lives not primarily by belief in a book or even a creed, but in a person—the Savior and Lord.

Why, then, the need to elaborate upon this simple assertion? Let us assume that we are asked what this affirmation means, *why* is Jesus the Lord? We would begin by affirming that he was a real person, human but more than human.

We would then, perhaps, be asked to explain what we mean by "Lord." In the Western world, which is increasingly moving away from authoritarian systems, it is difficult to talk about lords, except as parliamentary titles. Our lords today might be those who hold our mortgages or our employers.

The connective verb *is* suggests that somehow Jesus was not simply the lord of a two-thousand-year-old movement, but that he is Lord today. How? How does he still reign over us in a way that the great philosophers and teachers of the past do not?

The early Christians lived in a culture which had other lords and authorities. Both the Bible and the creeds emerged as ways to set forth the Christian understanding of the meaning of God's disclosure in

Christ and to define Christian faith against the speculative philosophies which surrounded it.

The Nicene Creed

As we noted earlier, the Apostles' Creed was a baptismal creed. It was so named because of the traditional belief that the apostles composed it. It was divided into three sections, dealing with Father, Son, and Holy Spirit. The Nicene Creed was formulated, in 325 A.D., at the Council of Nicea, a council called by Constantine to promote unity of belief among Christians. This council was preceded by controversy, much of which appears to us as rather tedious, but the issues at stake were of vital importance and the outcome was a good one for the church.

The controversy centered on the interpretation of the nature of Jesus Christ, the relation between his humanity and his divinity. Arius, a priest, had set forth the view that Jesus represented a kind of third gender made by God. The crucial word here is *made*, because Arius did not believe Jesus to possess the nature of God.

Athanasius, his adversary, insisted that Jesus was both divine and human. He rightly insisted that if Jesus did not experience a real humanity, but only seemed to (as the Gnostics believed), he could not be our savior, because to be our savior he must necessarily have experienced our nature. But if he possessed *only* a human nature, we would be without hope.

The Trinity

The Nicene Creed, traditionally said at the Eucharist, is composed of three parts (as is the Apostles' Creed), each of which confesses truths about each person of the Trinity.

The Trinity, as St. Thomas Aquinas notes, "is a holy mystery." Various analogies have been used to get at its meaning. St. Augustine approached it as the relationship between the lover (God) and the loved one (Christ), and the bond of love (Holy Spirit) between them. St. Patrick used the shamrock to explain to the Irish that God was one reality in three manifestations.

The doctrine of the Trinity is implicit in the New Testament. St. Paul repeatedly wrote, "The grace of our Lord Jesus Christ, the love of God, and the fellowship of the Holy Spirit be with us evermore." This suggests that in Christ we perceive a gracious God for, as St. Paul put it, "God was in Christ reconciling the world unto himself." The fellowship of the Holy Spirit is the invisible yet real presence of God.

The Trinity is a mystery but we live in the midst of mysteries. I knew my father first as companion—as he loved me, disciplined me, and sustained me. But as I grew older I came to realize that my existence was only possible because of him. Although separated by death, I continue in a spiritual way to sense his presence. An imperfect analogy, of course, but in a mysterious way the nature of the creative process—the artist, the work of art, and the spirit binding the two—is trinitarian, just as the lover, the loved one, and the bond between them is a trinity.

"One God in three persons" proves problematic for many, because we tend to think of persons as distinct individuals. The word *person* here, however, comes from the Latin *persona*, meaning "mask." In the Greek and Roman theater one actor would assume different roles and wear a mask for each character. The Christian affirmation of God is that he has three ways of being himself—Creator, Redeemer (in Christ), and Sanctifier (leading us into all truth and making us whole).

The first paragraph of the Nicene Creed affirms that God is Creator. Regardless of how we understand the process of creation, God created *ex nihilo*, "out of nothing." The second paragraph reveals our belief in Jesus Christ as begotten of God, "Very God of Very God." Thus while God created the world, he fathered his Son, who is of the substance of the Father.

This substance of God was "incarnate by the Holy Spirit of the Virgin Mary and was made man." Thus the Incarnation is crucial to doctrine, affirming the link between the Creator and his creation, the spiritual and the material finding hospitality in each other. As we noted in our study of Scripture, it is primarily about God's becoming man and thus being a definitive Word to us.

Ancient man had no problems with belief in virgin births. A story in the Jewish Midrash presents Moses as being born of a virgin, his birth accompanied by an unusual configuration of stars. The birth of Jesus is not mentioned in Gospels of Mark and John. In the Hebrew text of the Old Testament the word *almah*, meaning "young woman," was translated in the Septuagint version as *parthenos* which does mean "virgin." The early church used this latter translation.

Actually, the doctrine of the Virgin Birth was intended to safeguard the truth that Jesus was born of woman, to insist that his humanity was real and not apparent. While belief in Virgin Birth is an ancient act of faith, there is the alleged phenomenon of parthogenesis, birth without sexual intercourse.

However, the early apostolic preaching sets forth the uniqueness of Jesus by proclamation of his resurrection, not his birth. This is the primary miracle. It is that upon which Christianity stands or falls for, as St. Paul wrote, "If Christ has not been raised, then our preaching is in vain and your faith is in vain" (I Corinthians 15:14).

Scripture affirms that the Holy Spirit was the agent through which God brought a unique expression of himself into being, certainly through the cooperation of Mary,

> . . . and the power of the Most High
> will overshadow you;
> therefore the child to be born
> will be called holy,
> the Son of God (Luke 1:35).

Reference to the crucifixion follows. Here again it was important to the early church to proclaim that he really "suffered, died, and was buried" under a particular governor at a particular time. Unlike the prologue to so many fairy tales, there is no vague "once upon a time."

The final section of the middle part of the creed affirms his resurrection and coming again. "He ascended into heaven" is another problematic (to modern man) statement. As with the Virgin Birth, so here we have available in the annals of psychic mysteries accounts of levitation (practitioners of transcendental meditation allege such experiences).

But surely ascension means more here than levitation into space; to ascend really means to assume greater authority. Promotion, in our experience, means to assume wider responsibilities. When St. Paul writes in the first chapter of Ephesians that Christ was raised from the dead and sits "at his [God's] right hand in the heavenly places, far above all rule and authority and power and dominion . . .," he reflects this conviction and the true meaning of ascension.

I have read various attempts to provide rational and natural explanations for the mysteries of faith described above. In some cases these explanations reflect the presuppositions of their authors, presuppositions of a particular time. Ironically, attempts to explain away miracles often require one's having at least as much faith in these explanations as in the original events themselves! Our increasing discoveries of the dynamic relationship between mind and matter, exhibiting the power of the human spirit and psyche, have gone beyond the too neatly explained assumptions about what is *really* possible advanced in former times.

The concluding paragraph of the Nicene Creed states four great "I believes." The first of these has to do with the Holy Spirit, described as "the Lord and Giver of life." The Spirit of Christ is identified with the Spirit of God in creation. The Spirit inspired the prophets. The Spirit is the agent of continuing revelation and truth.

Perhaps the reason why belief in the Holy Spirit precedes the other great "I believes" lies in the statement of St. Paul: "No one can say 'Jesus is Lord' except by the Holy Spirit" (I Corinthians 12:3). That is, the truths of revelation can be believed and absorbed, not by human reason, but by the gift of the Spirit to lead us into these truths.

The second affirmation sets forth belief in the "one holy catholic and apostolic church." "Catholic" refers to the universal church which "proclaims the whole Faith to all people, to the end of time" (Prayer Book, p. 854). The church is apostolic because it "continues in the teaching and fellowship of the apostles and is sent to carry out Christ's mission to all people" (Prayer Book, p. 854).

The third affirmation sets forth belief in "one baptism" the purpose of which is the forgiveness of sins and incorporation into the community of faith. We are baptized but once and, as we saw earlier, baptism in water and in the name of the Trinity comprises a valid, and unrepeatable act. The Christian mission is not merely to provide educational and humanitarian services, but to baptize and to make disciples (Matthew 28:18).

The final great "I believe" will be noted in more detail in the last chapter, but what is important to note about this central affirmation of the faith is that it appears at the end of the Nicene Creed because it is the end or purpose of our faith. We come to believe in "the resurrection of the dead and the Life of the world to come" because the Holy Spirit (our first "I believe") raised Jesus from the dead; this testimony to his resurrection became the testimony which created and constituted one, holy, catholic, and apostolic church. We believe, then, *within* a community of faith, for the church in the power of the Holy Spirit nurtures and sustains faith.

The Nicene Creed arose from the church's attempt to find a way of expressing the nature of the human and divine in Christ. A familiar expression is "not one iota of difference." Literally only an *iota* (the Greek letter *i*) distinguished the views of Arius and Athanasius. Arius affirmed that Jesus was *homoiousios,* which meant that he was like God but not of the substance of God. Athanasius maintained that Jesus was *homoousios*, which meant of one substance with God. On one side of the issue was the view of Jesus as a divinely inspired prophet and on the other side was God incarnate to be worshiped.

The creeds are central to the study of Christology, the study of the person, attributes and life of Christ. With succeeding centuries, came more creeds, but basically they were all derived from the Nicene Creed. These creeds were written to counter what the church deemed heretical views. To mention but a few, Nestorius declared that there were two persons in Christ rather than two natures and Mary was the mother of his human nature only. Apollinarius denied that Jesus was fully human, claiming that his body was human but his spirit was not. The adoptionists taught that Jesus was a human prophet whose divinity was given to him when God adopted him at his baptism.

Most heresies are somewhat plausible because they are reflective of some truth, but a truth that is incomplete apart from the whole picture, a picture composed of mystery and paradox.

Essentially, creeds represent ways of bringing together, in a systematic statement, the truths of revelation in Scripture. Creeds are in reality the witness of Scripture brought into harmony. They are summaries of what the church believed Holy Scripture to declare concerning trinitarian truth.

The cause of "inclusive language" is ill served by those who would insist upon addressing God as "Father/Mother" or "parent," and the Son of God as "child." Because language shapes and conveys faith, these and other proposed substitutes for "Father" and "Son," point in a direction which may leave us with a god who is merely a concept instead of a specific Being. It is our faith that Jesus Christ, an actual historical person, was not begotten of a concept, nor was he fatherless. Words like Father, Son, and Lord are not just analogies out of our own experience, but are aspects and images of God's self revelation. Even as the first person of the Trinity is the Father of Jesus Christ, I believe that he is our Father, too. Since Mary, who represents the church, is the Mother of Jesus Christ then my maternal parent is Holy Mother Church. Admittedly, all three persons of the Trinity have both masculine and feminine characteristics, even as does the healthy church. Thus, we may faithfully say, "My God, my All!"

VII. The Church Year

Worship in the Episcopal Church, as in other churches in the liturgical tradition, is characterized by observance of particular seasons of what we call the "Christian Year" or the "Church Year." Not only are seasonal emphases observed, but also particular holy days or feast days.

Initially, this is somewhat bewildering to one who has not experienced this traditional cycle of observances. Just as the civil calendar has its special days, so does the church calendar.

The early church was built around the experience of the resurrection, the Easter Event. In the early church the word *pascha*—a Greek word derived from the Hebrew word *pesach*, meaning "passover"—was used. There is a saying in Judaism that "in every generation a man must so regard himself out of Egypt." The Christian perceived the resurrection as a new exodus. Although the Jewish Sabbath was celebrated on the seventh day of the week, the event of the resurrection on the first day of the week caused that day to become the primal holy day of the church.

The word *Easter* comes from an Anglo-Saxon word for the celebration of the goddess of spring. Each Sunday became a "little Easter." To keep the Sabbath day holy, meant for the first Christians to gather for the Eucharist which was the new Passover feast. Other seasons and holy days of the Christian year are determined by the date of Easter which is always "the first Sunday after the full moon, which happens upon or next after the twenty first day of March." There are, however, certain fixed dates such as Christmas and Epiphany.

During its first three centuries, the church celebrated the fifty days from Easter to Pentecost as a festival season. Pentecost means "fifty days." It was also the day celebrated, in the Jewish tradition, as thanksgiving for the harvest and the giving of the law to Moses. Ascension, which commemorates the departure of Christ to the Father, is celebrated forty days after Easter. On the day of Pentecost, as noted earlier, the church celebrates the outpouring and empowering presence of the Holy Spirit, sending the church forth into mission. Thus the primary event of Christian worship was Easter and, by extension, the continuing experience of the Holy Spirit. During this period the church scheduled baptism and confirmation.

In the fourth century what we know as Holy Week came into being. This was prompted, possibly, by the advent of pilgrimages into the Holy Land, the identification of the Mount of Calvary, the Holy Sepulchre, the Garden of Gethsemane, and the Mount of Olives. Following the period of persecution, the church had the leisure, given official recognition by the state, to erect monuments on those sites, and pilgrims appeared in succeeding times to retrace the route of our Lord's last week on earth.

In the late sixth century the season of Lent (including Holy Week) was established by Pope Gregory the Great. Lent (which comes into our language from an Anglo-Saxon word meaning "spring," "lengthening of days") signified a period of forty days, representative of our Lord's forty days of fasting in the desert prior to assuming his ministry. Themes of penitence and spiritual preparation became dominant in this season. Fasting, meaning abstinence from meat and a sparse intake of other food, characterized this period.

Lent begins with Ash Wednesday, so called because of the practice in ancient times of signing the foreheads of the faithful with an ashen cross. The ashes are those of the palms of the preceding Palm Sunday, representing acclamation of the Messiah. The ashes represent our mortality, the truth that "to dust we shall return." The sign of the cross foreshadows resurrection. This service includes a solemn Litany.

Next in point of development came the season celebrating the "Word made flesh," the festival of the Incarnation, called "Christmas"—"the Mass of Christ." Whereas the Easter festival is movable because, as is the case with Passover, it depends upon the lunar calendar, Christmas is fixed. The pagan appearance of the Sun god, reckoned on the solar year, is our date of December 25. It was the successful strategy of the church to undercut this pagan festival by supplanting it with the birth of "the Son of God."

A similar move was made with the feast of the Epiphany, from a Greek word meaning "manifestation." Epiphany celebrates the manifestation or appearance of Christ to the Gentiles, represented in the persons of the wise men or magi. This event was placed by the Eastern church on January 6, which was already a pagan holy day in observance of the birth of Osiris. During the fourth century, it passed into the tradition of the Western church.

The Puritans did not celebrate these festivals because of their pagan origins. Today some denominations follow the Puritan precedent by claiming that there is nothing in Scripture to justify their observance. Certainly no dates are mentioned in Scripture of the birth and resurrection of Christ. However, the early Christians believed that in Christ "there cannot be Greek and Jew . . . but Christ is all, and in all" (Colossians 3:11). The early Christians believed that in Jesus Christ the expectations, the hopes of pagan religions were in reality fulfilled. What they yearned for, the church provided, for Christianity was to be the universal fulfillment of all religions.

As with Easter, a period of preparation became prefixed to the Christmas event. This was Advent, the four weeks prior to Christmas. Advent means "coming" and, indeed, the tone of Advent is expectation and preparation. A favorite theme on Advent Sundays in the ancient church centered in "the four last things"—death, judgment, heaven, and hell. Advent reminds us that the coming One brings judgment as well as hope. The season of Advent has all but been obliterated by a Christmas season that, commercially, begins before Thanksgiving. While Advent is not a penitential season such as Lent, it can afford us with the spiritual opportunity to reflect upon the meaning of the coming One, the Messiah, thus representing an antidote for much of the self-indulgence that accompanies Christmas.

These seasons make up approximately half of the Christian year. From Advent to Pentecost there is a sense of the drama of our deliverance. Our Lord is anticipated, his birth is celebrated, his passion and death are shared, he is raised from the dead, he pours forth his Spirit upon all.

In the tenth century, the Sunday after Pentecost Sunday came to be known as Trinity Sunday, upon which day was celebrated God's manifestation as a triune being. In twelfth-century England, the Sundays extending from the beginning of summer through the late fall were called "Sundays after Trinity." Our present Prayer Book, however, follows the custom of listing these Sundays as Sundays "after Pentecost." This brings us into conformity with the ancient tradition which preferred to date Sundays after an event—in this case the event of the outpouring of the Spirit—rather than after a doctrine, as was the case with Trinity Sunday. During the season of Pentecost, which comprises about half the Christian year, we reflect primarily upon the teachings of Jesus and the universal implications of the gospel.

Finally, the church calendar commemorates the saints. In popular understanding a saint is someone of exemplary heroism and virtue, given this status either because of the sacrifice of life or the performance of miracles. In the New Testament, however, the word applies to all Christians, many of whom indeed gave up life and property for their commitment. A saint is one of God's people, participating in the community of faith.

The Prayer Book lists as saints the apostles and evangelists who were the first witnesses to our Lord. Certain days on the calendar are set aside for them. Each saint's day has its own prayer and lessons for the Eucharist. In 1963 the Episcopal Church published a book entitled *Lesser Feasts and Fasts* (revised in 1973). Included are saints who were missionaries, theologians, pastors, and Christians of exemplary significance extending into modern times.

Throughout the Anglican Communion, the various churches have their own heritage of saints, missionaries, priests, teachers, and bishops. These are not formally canonized in the way the process is used in the Roman Catholic Church, but they have emerged by consensus over a period of time. Many of our saints' days and holy days are those of the Roman Catholic and Orthodox Churches.

A word about the use of the various colors. Advent and Lent, seasons of preparation and penitence, are marked by the use of purple. This color (in ancient times derived from a costly dye) signifies royalty and mourning. White represents purity—festivals of joy, weddings, Christmas, Easter, and days commemorating certain feasts of our Lord, such as the Transfiguration. Red signifies martyrdom and is frequently used on saints' days, although it is used at Pentecost to signify the tongues of fire. Green, used during Epiphany and the Sundays after Pentecost, represents the universal color of life and growth.

The church calendar dramatizes the cycle of the recurring truths of our faith, putting us in touch with the "old, old, story" ever made new. The church year, in its rich variety of lessons, anthems, prayers, and colors, exposes us to the vast sweep of the movement of God toward us so that we may be lifted up to him.

VIII. Prayer and the Prayer Book

Of all the religious acts in which we involve ourselves, the act of prayer is the most difficult for modern man. In fact, I'm not so sure that it was much easier for ancient or biblical man. Certainly the picture we get of our Lord praying in the garden of Gethsemane before his crucifixion is one of struggle before resolve and surrender. Jesus well knew the cry of the Psalmist, "Turn thou to me, and be gracious to me; for I am lonely and afflicted" (Psalm 25:16). The implication here is that it is possible for God to turn away from us, to answer us by his silence—not a comforting thought to us today, who live in a time of sophisticated communication, when we can make contact with space ships approaching distant planets. How can contact with God be assured?

If unanswered prayer is a problem for us, answered prayer is also a problem. A few years ago Kris Kristofferson wrote a hit entitled "Why Me, Lord?" The song describes the experience of God's undeserved grace. Why me and not someone else? Or, conversely, why do my non-religious and irreligious friends seem to prosper, but I, who pray, am left with unresolved problems? This was noted also by the Psalmist, who frequently spoke of the prosperity of the unrighteous. All kinds of testimonies about prayer are available on tape and in books in ever-increasing numbers, everything from "the Lord sold my house for me" to cures for terminal illnesses.

Thus answered and unanswered prayer invites questions of God: "My God, my God, why hast thou forsaken me?" (Psalm 22:1). Does God abandon us, does he "answer" us with silence, or is his answer "No, not yet"? Are we blessed in proportion to our goodness, righteousness, or spirituality? Is prayer ultimately a technique, a means of using the right words at the right time in the right state of grace, catching God when he is in, and thus effecting the blessings we desire?

Or is prayer simply and ultimately a kind of dialogue with ourselves, a means of getting in touch with our inner resources, of tapping hidden powers within us, leading us to the realization of our potential?

I have included in the bibiography books which deal with these questions—certainly beyond limitations of space here; but I should note that, increasingly, our church is providing opportunities for us to pray together, to share our experience of prayer, even the periods of darkness described in the rich heritage of the mystics with their "dark night of the soul." We are coming to appreciate the truth expressed by Isaiah when he speaks of "the treasures of darkness" (Isaiah 45:3), implying that spiritual depression is a normal part of the Christian life from time to time.[1]

There are many excellent books of prayers, books on prayer, and books telling us how to pray. But for the Episcopalian there is one book that is the greatest of them all—the Book of Common Prayer. John Wesley said of the Prayer Book, "I know no book that breathes a more rational, solid, Scriptural piety than the Common Prayer of the Church of England. ...." Louis Boyer, a Roman Catholic theologian, has said that it represents "not only one of the most impressive, but also one of the purest forms of Christian Common Prayer to be found in the world." Our present book is even richer in its resources than its predecessors.

As for praying "out of a book," it must be said that the Prayer Book is not intended to be a substitute for the personal prayers out of our hearts, with eyes closed if so desired. (I recall a seminary professor in another denomination saying "What's the difference between reading a prayer from a book and reading it off the back of your eyelids?")

We sing together from a common hymnal; we offer the Psalms together from a common Psalter. Thus prayer at public worship is something we are invited to do together, for the Prayer Book is a means of unifying our intercessions, our adoration, and thanksgiving. Prayer is not just "a flight from the alone to the Alone," but characterizes the purpose of the gathered community of Christians. When our Lord taught his disciples to pray, he taught them a prayer beginning, "*Our Father.*"

There is an old saying, "the Prayer Book protects the people from the priesthood," which means that the priest or lay leader of worship is subject to this standard. There is also a sense in which the Prayer Book protects the people from getting lost in their own personal needs. A primary hazard of prayer is that it often becomes colored by our own needs. Our Prayer Book states that "prayer is offered with intercession for the Universal Church, . . . the Nation and all in authority, the welfare of the world, the concerns of the local community, those who suffer and those in any trouble, the departed . . ." (Prayer Book, p. 383).

The classic kinds of prayer are set forth in the Prayer Book: Petition, prayers of asking; Thanksgiving, which requires us to give thanks whether we feel thankful or not; Intercession, prayer for others; and finally Adoration, the loftiest form of prayer, wherein we adore God not for what he gives us but for who he is.

Consider the prayer that begins the Eucharist. This kind of prayer is called a collect. Collects, which comprise a great part of our prayers, are so called because they "collect" our thoughts and aspirations around a particular theme.

> Almighty God, unto whom all hearts are open, all desires known, and from whom no secrets are hid; Cleanse the thoughts of our hearts by the inspiration of thy Holy Spirit, that we may perfectly love thee, and worthily magnify thy holy name, through Christ our Lord. *Amen*

This collect begins with an ascription; it notes one of God's attributes—that he knows us. The heart of the collect is the petition asking him to help us worship him by cleansing our thoughts through the inspiration of his Holy Spirit. This is sound doctrine at the heart of every collect and prayer, and the doctrine here is that it is God who makes worship possible. God is both the object and source of praise and worship. "Through Christ our Lord" reminds us that every prayer is offered through him.

We can say this collect like any other in our own words. Yet it is difficult to improve upon the economy of expression and simple directness of the collects. We make them ours by saying "amen" at the end ("so be it"), and this is the response not of the priest or lay leader but the congregation.

Familiarity with the prayers of the Prayer Book provides the resources to enable us to pray spontaneously. When our Lord cried out, "My God, my God, why have you forsaken me?" he was quoting Psalm 22, from his Prayer Book, the Psalter.

There is a saying which bears crucial significance for the Episcopalian: "As we pray, so we believe." There are denominations which emphasize doctrine and confessions of faith as their standards. But what we believe is set forth in *how* we pray, for it is the Prayer Book providing common prayer and worship, more so than assent to doctrine, which characterizes the Episcopalian. We are constituted by our common prayer. What is important to us is not that we believe everything in the same way but that we pray together. Surely it is only out of a life of prayer that doctrine, dogma, discipline, and creed can find meaning and expression.

The History of the Prayer Book

Revision of the Prayer Book has never been without controversy. In 1549 the appearance of the first Prayer Book caused rioting, one lady hurling a chair through a stained glass window in St. Giles Cathedral, Edinburgh. The 1552 Prayer Book, which expressed a predominantly Protestant bias, angered many.

Under Elizabeth I, the Prayer Book was again revised. It represented a compromise of the 1549 and 1552 books. Cromwell had it outlawed by Parliament and a Puritan *Directory of Worship* was put in its place—a dour and gloomy thing.

In 1662, Charles II reinstated the Prayer Book, this time with the notable provision of including prayers for the dead in the Holy Communion service. This book is still the standard for the Church of England.

Following the American Revolution, at the organization of the American Episcopal Church in 1789, the English Prayer Book was revised in light of the needs of the American Church. Following this revision, there was one in 1892 and then again in 1928.

The history of the Prayer Book revision is a fascinating study. The principle of revision has always been operative in our church. In the preface of the 1928 book we note, "yet upon the principles laid down, it cannot but be supposed that further alterations would in time be found expedient."

The 1928 revision appeared without trial usage. Our present book was authorized for trial usage in 1970. While this process created confusion and anger, it also led, because of the experience of widespread use, to helpful changes. While many wished to be spared this experience, there were those who believed that trial usage enabled them to rethink what had often become simply rote and habitual in worship.

Certainly the case for a cautious approach to liturgical change is not without merit. The value of ritual is assurance. Episcopalians prefer the predictable. We hunger for permanence amid the plastic, disposable, throwaway culture of "planned obsolescense." Conservatives remind us of the tyranny of the contemporary and offer a needed critique of our mania for the modern. But the case for revision has its side in the truth that today's traditions were yesterday's innovations. Indeed, when hymns were introduced they were denounced as a departure from plainsong.

On the whole, our present Prayer Book represents the fruits of solid liturgical study. Just as the translators of the King James Version of the Bible did not have access to some important manuscripts which we now have, in our present century scholars have also given us increased knowledge of worship in the Apostolic and Patristic ages of the church.

While much of the 1928 book is informed by devotional material of the late Middle Ages, the present book, more than its predecessor, sets forth the great themes of Incarnation, Atonement, Resurrection, and Ascension. In a real sense, the new book is conservative in its offering of pre-medieval liturgies.

It represents in its "Rite I" forms the best of our heritage of Elizabethan English but gives us in "Rite II" forms in more modern English. Thus the essential beauty of the traditional Book of Common Prayer is no more in danger of being lost to civilized people than the King James Bible.

Those who bemoan the presence of modern English pointedly observe that archaic language, with its suggestion of mystery and the "awesome," lifts us to the Holy, the "otherworldly."

Those who press for translation and simplification correctly observe that the literature of the New Testament was not in classical Greek but in the common Greek of the day. Certainly Archbishop Cranmer successfully rendered the language of worship and prayer into the English of his century.

Our present Prayer Book represents the Anglican genius for holding truths in tension. Certainly the archaic, whether it be expressed in Elizabethan English, Latin, or Greek, can imply the holy and the transcendent. We can sense the presence of the holy without understanding the language about the holy.

The other truth is that, if liturgy is literally "the work of the people," language is important. An informal Eucharist around a dining room table or a folk mass with guitars and simple songs can afford participation in an experience of God who is not just "high and lifted up" (Isaiah 6:1ff.), but a God in the midst of his people. A picnic, just as Christmas dinner with linen and silver, is a ritual of the family.

The danger present in both life and liturgy is that we can so easily become captive either of the traditional or the contemporary. When our Hymnal was revised in 1940, the editors stated a principle applicable to all revision: "Prove all things, hold fast to that which is good."

The Design of the Prayer Book

Because of the availability of recent books which serve as excellent study guides of Prayer Book content, I will deal only briefly with basic components.[2]

While a book of prayer, the Prayer Book sets forth the services of the church, the Psalter, lectionaries, or schedules listing the selection of appropriate Scripture for public and private worship, historical documents, and an Outline of the Faith—a redesign of the traditional Catechism.

The Daily Office

Following the Preface there is a statement "Concerning the Service of the Church." It begins with:

> The Holy Eucharist, the principal act of Christian worship on the Lord's Day and other major Feasts, and Daily Morning and Evening Prayer, as set forth in this Book, are the regular services appointed for public worship in this Church.

Then follows the Calendar of the Church Year, setting forth the principal holy days and seasons.

An "office" is another name for an act of worship, either public or private. As with the Eucharist, the Daily Office appears in a Rite I form and a Rite II form. The Daily Office is a composite of Scripture, the recitation of Psalms, the Apostles' Creed, and a series of prayers, which can be drawn not just from the selections in the office but from any place in the book. A selection of canticles—Scripture set to music—is provided. A sermon may be given.

The Daily Office, so called because of the tradition that Morning and Evening Prayer are daily acts of worship either public or private, had its origin in the synagogue services of morning, afternoon, and evening prayer.

Monastic prayer and worship featured seven periods of prayer in which Psalms, Old and New Testament readings, canticles, and prayers were used. The genius of Archbishop Cranmer in the sixteenth century is demonstrated in his revision of these monastic offices into the two services of Morning and Evening Prayer. Some Episcopal churches today have these services daily, or one of them daily, or feature them in Advent and/or Lent. A lay reader may read them. Many churches without priests avail themselves of the Daily Office on Sundays. The Daily Office, however, was never intended to supplant (as it has done in places) the Eucharist as the principal act of worship. Some parishes combine part of Morning or Evening Prayer with the Eucharist.

Following the Daily Offices are brief services for Noonday, an order of worship for the Evening, and Compline—all representing parts of the ancient offices. "Daily Devotions for Individuals and Families" further enriches possibilities for briefer, less formal periods of prayer and meditation.

The Great Litany and the Collects

Litany is derived from a Greek word which means "to pray." In the 1549 Prayer Book it was the first service to be translated into English. Here it is retained in its majestic English with intercessions added for the lonely and other needy. It is an appropriate act of worship during Lent or during times of crisis. (Because of its highly participatory nature, the redoubtable Puritan patriarch Cotton Mather once spoke of it as a tennis game between the minister and the congregation.) Other litanies of varying kinds are provided.

The "Collects for the Church Year" are printed in two forms—traditional and contemporary language. The collects comprise one part of what we call "the propers." Each Sunday or special day and season has its "proper" selection of Scripture and collect.

Following the collects is a section entitled "Proper Liturgies for Special Days." These are for Ash Wednesday, Palm Sunday, Maundy Thursday, Good Friday, Holy Saturday, and the Great Vigil of Easter. Again, they represent the inclusion of ancient liturgies adapted for worship today.

Holy Baptism

Holy Baptism, while printed at the beginning of "the Pastoral Offices" in the 1928 book, now precedes the liturgies of the Eucharist to emphasize that it is through baptism that we come to the Lord's table. This service is designed for both infant and adult baptism. It is clear that, usually, baptism is to be "administered within the Eucharist as the chief service on a Sunday or other feast." The nature of this service, with its incorporation of "the Baptismal Covenant," is intended to provide a renewal of the congregation's baptismal vows, thus involving members of the congregation as participants rather than spectators. Provision is made for the use of oil of Chrism, blessed by the bishop.

The Holy Eucharist

Regardless of the method of celebrating the Eucharist—that is, the ritual used—its basic composition has been the same since ancient times. One should distinguish between liturgy and ritual. Liturgy involves the essential things that need to be done, while ritual describes the varying ways we may do them. Let us note the four sections of this liturgy, the same in all liturgical churches.

"The Word of God" includes the opening affirmations and collects, the lessons, sermon, and Nicene Creed. In this first section we are engaged primarily in hearing, in instruction and edification.

"The Prayers of the People" follow, with various options or forms of prayer being offered. These may include an act of confession, or a separate confession may follow, but in this section we offer our adoration, petition, intercession, and thanksgiving.

"The Great Thanksgiving" is the third and most dramatic aspect of the Eucharist. Here the drama of salvation is recited, the bread and wine blessed. This is preceded not only by the offering of bread and wine (often by laity from the congregation), but by the offering of our alms and pledges, thus dramatizing that all is from God. These are blessed in order to be instruments and means of his presence. In the early church people brought food and clothing for the needy to the altar at this point.

Prior to the drama of the Great Thanksgiving, we are invited to greet each other in the name of the Lord by saying "The peace of the Lord be with you," which may be accompanied by other words of greeting and welcome. Our Lord told us that the offering of any gift at the altar should be preceded by an act of reconciliation (Matthew 5:23). This act represents the restoration of one of the most ancient parts of the liturgy. It also affords a kind of intermission, a moment of informality before the sacred prayers of the consecration of the bread and the wine.

The final section of the Eucharist is the "Breaking of the Bread," followed by the reception of Holy Communion. In the ancient church the bread was broken not just for symbolical reasons, but for the practical purpose of distributing it. The large host or wafer is broken by the priest to signify that once we ate from the same loaf. Today leavened bread is often used. Being a communicant involves sharing in the holy mystery of the presence of Christ and hence with each other, to go out refreshed into the world to become the church in mission.

As with the Prayers of the People, the Great Thanksgiving is given in various forms, some of them representative of ancient liturgies, and some of them of new liturgies. Each of these prayers sets forth the drama of our redemption, noting not only the sacrifice of Christ, but the themes of Creation, Incarnation, the descent of the Spirit, and his coming again.

While at the heart of the liturgy there is the priest *taking* bread and wine, setting them apart to become the presence of Christ, *blessing* the symbols of our existence, *offering* them up, and *breaking* the bread, the gathered congregation is also deeply involved in helping to *make* Eucharist.

The Pastoral Offices

Confirmation, Marriage, Thanksgiving for Children, Ministry to the Sick, Reconciliation of a Penitent, and Christian Burial are included in the next section.

The service of Confirmation provides not only for that act which we have discussed earlier, but for the reception and the reaffirmation of baptismal vows. The bishop's visitation may also include his laying on of hands and prayer with those who have particular needs. "A Form of Commitment to Christian Service" is appropriate to those beginning some ministry in the church, teaching, serving on the vestry, etc. Again, this manifests the need for the continuing strengthening presence of the Holy Spirit.

The "Celebration and Blessing of a Marriage" is not radically different than in preceding Prayer Books. Included are more selections from Scripture and additional prayers. The bride and the groom may select the Scripture and provide the bread and wine for the Eucharist, which is emphasized as a part of the wedding, unlike former books. The formula, "With this ring I thee wed . . .," has been replaced by "(name), I give you this ring as a symbol of my vow, and with all that I am, and all that I have I honor you, in the name of God." This effectively captures the old promise (deleted from the 1928 book by Victorian hands), "With my body I thee worship, and with my worldly goods I thee endow." "The Blessing of a Civil Marriage" is included to provide a ministry to those who have not been married in the church.

"A Thanksgiving for the Birth or Adoption of a Child" follows. The somewhat gloomy language of the 1928 book, reflecting the "great peril and pain of childbirth," has been dropped. This service is derived in the main from the ancient Jewish service of the purification of women, but its emphasis is upon thanksgiving, involving the family and the congregation. The service for the adoption of a child, not provided in past books, has met with wide acceptance.

"The Reconciliation of a Penitent," given in two rites, has experienced wide acceptance. Prior books gave permission for confession to a priest, but no forms were provided. This rite is prefaced by the statement that "Another Christian may be asked to hear a confession, but it must be made clear to the penitent that absolution will not be pronounced; instead, a declaration of forgiveness is provided." An essential function of priesthood is the pronouncement of absolution, derived from our Lord's commission to the apostles, "Whose sins you forgive they are forgiven. . . ." Absolution is contingent upon a true confession.

In regard to private or sacramental confession, there is an old Anglican saying, "All may; none must; some should." We will see later how essential this is to healing. Even in the 1928 book, the service of "Visitation of the Sick" includes, "then shall the sick person be moved to make a special confession of his sins, if he feel his conscience troubled with any matter . . ." (p. 313).

The service of "Ministration to the Sick" is divided into three parts: the "Ministry of the Word," "Laying on of Hands and Anointing," and Holy Communion. This is followed by a service of "Ministration at the Time of Death." These services, while conforming to preceding books, are enriched by additional passages of Scripture. Particularly helpful are the "Prayers for a Vigil."

"The Burial of the Dead" is given in two rites: Rite I continues the tradition of preceding books and Rite II enriches this tradition. All of the beloved prayers of the past which have made this service so impressive to non-Episcopalians, as well as comforting to those in our tradition of faith, are there. Prayers in a litany form are provided for use at the Eucharist (called a "requiem"), and anthems are provided as the body is borne from the church.

"The Ordinal," which represents the services for the ordination of deacons, priests, and bishops, follows. These services have their origin in the ordination rites described in the *Apostolic Tradition,* a document of the second century.

The "Celebration of a New Ministry" is described for the institution of the rector of a parish or for anyone assuming any kind of ministry within the parish. A service for "the Dedication and Consecration of a Church" follows.

We now come to the Psalter or Psalms, many of which were written by David. The Psalter has been called the "Hymnal of the Second Temple," dating from around 450 B.C. Praise, penitence, lament, thanksgiving, and prophecies pointing to our Lord provide its themes. The Psalms may be chanted or said. Notes relevant to their present translation are provided.

The section of prayers and thanksgiving (pages 810–841) includes many from preceding books as well as the addition of ancient ones, for example, the beloved prayer attributed to St. Francis. New prayers are here. There are prayers for the lonely and the addicted, prayers for peace and the stewardship of natural resources.

An essential component of the Prayer Book has always been the Catechism. The word *Catechism* is taken from a Greek word meaning "to ring out," and it refers to the response of those asked questions concerning the faith. It has been revised as "An Outline of the Faith," designed to make it more appropriate for congregational participation.

The old Catechism was followed by: "And all Fathers, Mothers, Masters, and Mistresses, shall cause their Children, Servants, and Apprentices, who have not learned their Catechism, to come to the Church at the time appointed . . ." (Book of Common Prayer, 1928, p. 582).

Deleted from the earlier Catechism are such responses as, for example, to the question of duty towards neighbor, "To submit myself to all my governors. . . . To order myself lowly and reverently to all my betters. . . . to keep my hands from picking and stealing."

The content of Christian education is set forth in simple and direct language. "What is Prayer?" is followed by the response, "Prayer is responding to God, by thought and by deeds, with or without words" (p. 856).

The section, "Historical Documents of the Church," is inclusive of material not found in the 1928 book. Herein is found the Creed of St. Athanasius and the classic statement on the union of the divine and human natures in Christ, formulated in 451 A.D. at the Council of Chalcedon. Of particular interest is the inclusion of the Preface of the first Book of Common Prayer (1549). It begins with the statement, "There was never anything by the wit of man so well devised, or so sure established, which in continuance of time hath not been corrupted . . ." (p. 866).

The "Articles of Religion" or "the Thirty-Nine Articles" (and "The Chicago-Lambeth Quadrilateral 1886, 1888") conclude this section. These articles were composed in the sixteenth century under Elizabeth I. Just as the creeds were occasioned by the presence of conflict and confusion in regard to proper doctrine, so the Thirty-Nine Articles emerged as an attempt by the Church of England to express its position in contradistinction to the Puritan movement and the Roman Catholic faith.

These articles have traditionally served as a standard of doctrine and faith. However, with any standard there can be, as in the law, strict constitutionalists as well as those whose interpretations are more liberal in scope. There are denominations which require absolute adherence to particular confessions of faith; deviation may well mean deposition or excommunication. In the American tradition, the candidate for ordination to the priesthood is not asked to swear loyalty to the Thirty-Nine Articles as such, but rather to the faith of the church, expressed in Scripture and creed, with the promise to uphold the discipline of the church.

Thus the articles are not objects of faith, written on stone tablets to bind future generations. The Articles of Faith sought to define who we were and what we believed as over against competing alternatives. They exhibit the controversies of the times.

To cite but one example: Article twenty-eight states that "The Sacrament of the Lord's Supper was not by Christ's ordinance reserved, carried about, lifted up, or worshipped." This was written in reaction to what many perceived to be superstitious uses of the sacrament. To follow this article literally would mean that Holy Communion could not be reserved for the sick, or that those churches featuring the service of "Benediction" (where prayers are said in adoration of the sacrament) would have to cease such devotions. There are Episcopalians who prefer to adhere literally to this article, and those who, while approving reservation of the consecrated sacrament for purposes of visitation to the sick, disapprove strongly of reservation for devotional reasons.

The abuse of something does not preclude the possibility of its proper use. One can believe in the supernatural—God present and adored in the Sacrament of the altar—without succumbing to superstition. From my observation, most of the superstitions of our time (the occult) are found outside of the church.

In our time, we are experiencing in large measure release from the defensive, reactive postures of times past. The Roman Catholics have moved far beyond the reactive teachings of the Council of Trent. In all major denominations we perceive a willingness to explore types of worship which may not have historically characterized that denomination. We can be devoted to enduring truths of our various heritages without being dominated by them, for the work of the Holy Spirit cannot be claimed exclusively by any one tradition.

The concluding section of the Prayer Book is "the Lectionary." Previous books provided a schedule of readings from the Psalms and the Old and New Testaments for each Sunday, each Holy Day, and the days of the week. The present Book sets forth a schedule of readings in three cycles: Year A, Year B, and Year C. This insures far more exposure to Scripture than did previous lectionaries. Readings for the Daily Office—Year One and Year Two—contribute to this increased inclusion.

While various schedules or plans of reading Scripture are available from various sources, for the Episcopalian the lectionary of the Prayer Book is to be used because it relates the reading of Scripture to the seasons of the church year.

IX. The Church's Discipline

All institutions are characterized by a *discipline*, a word which carries the connotation of that which is punitive and restrictive. The word, however, comes from *disciple*. To be a disciple is, by definition, to be under discipline. The teachings and traditions of the church nourish, correct, and enhance the life of the disciple. Within the church the presence of the Teacher is still mediated through worship, learning, and discipline.

It usually comes as a surprise to new Episcopalians that the minimum requirement for a communicant in "good standing" is the reception of Holy Communion three times a year. While attendance at divine worship is assumed, our church does not officially define absence from worship as a sin. The Episcopal Church has tended to avoid the somewhat militant pronouncements about church attendance heard in other denominations. The Episcopal Church has rightly noted that, as we grow in our knowledge and love of God, the discipline of the church, including the discipline of attendance on the Lord's Day, becomes an invitation rather than an invasion of our person.

This chapter will present prayer, fasting, giving, marriage, healing, and death as areas of Christian experience to which the discipline of the church speaks.

Prayer

The existence of a Prayer Book is in itself an example of prayer as a discipline. It is the supreme act of discipleship, for it effects communion between the disciple and the Teacher—our Lord Jesus Christ. He told his disciples that they "ought always to pray" (Luke 18:1). Prayer is offered not because we feel like praying. There is no technique to prayer, whereby it becomes the means of getting us what we want or deliverance from what we do not want. Søren Kierkegaard wrote, in one of his journals, that the person who prays continues to pray not in order for God to hear what is being prayed for, but so that the one praying may hear what it is that God has to say to him.

One of the most helpful books on prayer in recent years was written by Jacques Ellul, a lay theologian and former leader in the French resistance. He presents a critique of the reasons often given for praying and not praying, noting that, while there is some truth to the old saying that "work is prayer," hence what we do is prayer, the reverse is most crucial to the life of prayer: "The Catholic Church in her wisdom knew that to work is precisely not to pray, and that it was necessary to interrupt work in order to stand for a while before the Lord, to offer up the work done or to be done."[1] It is his thesis that the disciple prays not for the payoff of prayer, or necessarily for any reason, except that he is commanded to pray.

The setting apart of a time and place is important, a time that is ours, kept with the same seriousness as we would keep any important appointment. We need a place where we can keep before us the devotional classics of the masters. We have often heard it said that "God is everywhere," but a God who is everywhere can soon become a God who is nowhere. The ancient Jews knew this; that is why they built the Temple and set aside time and space sacred to prayer so that all times and places could manifest the presence of God.

While frequently prayer may emerge spontaneously, it is first and foremost a discipline. When the disciples asked our Lord to teach them to pray, he gave them a prayer—what we have come to call "the Lord's Prayer." To pray for our "daily bread" clearly implies that we are to offer this prayer up daily.

Fasting

To some, fasting implies the piety of fanatics sitting on pillars; fasting implies a kind of "starvathon" (to coin a word) which is perceived to be a means of salvation. In a secular sense, fasting in the sense of a "hunger strike" has proved effective in changing prison policies. It has been used to dramatize world hunger. Churches of all denominations are tending to encourage meatless Wednesdays, Fridays, and other days, not simply as acts of personal piety, but to dramatize the plight of millions who have no food.

Lent and Ember Days (at which time increase of the ministry is prayed for) and Fridays have been observed by many Episcopalians as days of fasting. Fasting may mean only one full meal a day, a sparse intake at all meals, or abstinence from meat. Ash Wednesday and Good Friday are noted in the Prayer Book as days on which fasting is required. On Sundays and Holy Days fasting may be foregone, because these days are feast days. During Lent fasting may involve the giving up of tobacco, desserts, alcohol or other staples of survival for many!

Fasting is a part of all religions and, while there are humanitarian reasons for fasting—for the Christian fasting—like prayer, lies in the example and teaching of our Lord. Before our Lord began his ministry, he was driven by the Spirit into the wilderness to encounter Satan. His fasting enabled him to manifest spiritual clarity in the midst of temptation. Traditionally, then, for the disciple fasting often precedes some mission or task. On one occasion, when his disciples were unable to effect a healing, Jesus noted that what was needed was not only prayer but fasting (Matthew 17:21).

Periodically, I find it important to fast before I enter into what I suspect will be a difficult counseling session or the hearing of a confession which I suspect will be a painful one. Apart from the value of fasting to dramatize self-denial in a society built on overabundance or for other humanitarian reasons, fasting is commended for the sake of the soul, to enable spiritual clarity in the presence of the powers of this world.

Giving

Giving and stewardship are sometimes associated with the process of shaking the sheckels out of the faithful and the not so faithful—the Every Member Canvass. I have noted that this subject, more so than many others, has a way of occasioning anger, because money represents one of the deepest anxieties we can experience. Nearly one-sixth of all the teachings of Jesus have to do with money and stewardship of other resources God has given us.

In Matthew 6:24ff. and Luke 16:9ff., Jesus speaks of money as being under the power of Mammon, the god of money. The tithe in the Old Testament (which I believe is assumed in the New Testament) was not given just to maintain the Temple and the priesthood, but it was a ritual offering to insure the consecration of all of one's financial and material resources. To put it another way, if one could not ritually offer a sacrificial percentage, he would come under the dominion, the power, of money. He would, in effect, become possessed by his possessions. I have discovered that, without exception, a person who gives generously to a God who has given the supremely generous gift of his Son is one who no longer is anxious about money. He is delivered from its dominion over his life.

Our Lord said, ". . . where your treasure is, there will your heart be also" (Matthew 6:21). We are committed to the future of those things in which we have invested not only our money, but our time and talent.

The Episcopal Church has traditionally avoided legalism in this matter. Some members of my parish give ten percent of their gross income, some ten percent of their net income, some exceed ten percent in both categories. What is important is growth in giving. Throughout the Episcopal Church a standard is emerging whereby we are invited to give $1.00 per week per $1,000 dollars of income, which comes out to about five percent of our income. Certainly a healthy church budget should not be the sole object of Christian giving for God accomplishes his purposes through other agencies.

The giving of money, time, and talent are not means of earning God's love, but rather of responding to that love and expressing it materially. The disciple is under a discipline to give.

Holy Matrimony

Perhaps it seems strange to the reader that marriage has anything to do with Christian discipline or discipleship. However, in the Christian faith the giving of two people to each other, with the promised commitments, assumes that marriage represents a "calling" or vocation, a way in which discipleship can be effectively maintained. At the same time, celibacy is also an act of discipleship, a calling.

Many Episcopalians and non-Episcopalians have collided with the discipline of our church on their intent either to be married for the first time or to be remarried after divorce. In both cases it is the policy of the Episcopal Church to require in-depth marital counseling by the priest. Customarily, no date for the wedding is set until this process is complete. Many clergy have seen engagements broken after revelations which have emerged in premarital counseling, revelations which cast serious doubt upon the readiness of those to be married.

Permission for the marriage of a divorced person is known as a "Godly Judgment," and is given by a bishop only upon recommendation by a priest. Customarily, a year's time from the date of the divorce decree is required. (There are obvious reasons for this, centering on the wisdom of avoiding "rebound" marriages.) Prior to any marriage a thirty-day waiting period is required.

The Episcopal Church has always recognized the presence of factors in a marriage which could nullify it. For example, incest, "mistaken identity," failure to have reached puberty, "mental deficiency of either party sufficient to prevent the exercise of intelligent choice." Also, if either party disclosed for the first time after the marriage an unwillingness to have children, this would be grounds to have the marriage annulled; whereas our church does not require the promise to have children, it does insist that neither spouse be confronted by a surprise.

Before a marriage, the couple signs a statement called a "Declaration of Intent," which declares, among other things, the conviction that the marriage is to be lifelong. Traditionally, given the existence of divorces, a painful dilemma was presented. If the grounds for divorce did not coincide with any of the grounds for nullification, in the eyes of the church the marriage, although a bad one, still existed. On the other hand, there has been the option of being remarried either in a civil ceremony or by clergy of another denomination. Persons remarried in this fashion, after a period of time in which they evidenced regular attendance in an Episcopal Church, could petition for a Godly Judgment, have their marriage blessed, and return to the full sacramental life of the church. Prior to 1973 this meant that divorced persons could receive the sacraments but, upon remarriage outside of our church, they effectively excommunicated themselves. However, after a period of time, they could receive a Godly Judgment. Many, understandably, never came back.

This procedure was in many ways more punitive than pastoral in that the sacramental life of the church was often witheld during a time when the couple needed it. It was dishonest in that it forced clergy to bootleg marriages, that is, while denying that a remarriage could be valid in the Episcopal Church, it was assumed that a remarriage could, in fact, take place elsewhere.

The General Convention of 1973 revised the marriage canons, recognizing that relationships can and do spiritually die. It has been my experience and that of other clergy that many of the couples we counsel who seek remarriage were never counseled before their first marriage. Wrong motives and false expectations, which needed only time and crises to emerge, were present. In a similar sense, men have left the priesthood upon finally realizing that they sought holy orders for the wrong reason or were simply unable to cope with that role.

Any proposed remarriage must require, for the bishop's Godly Judgment, evidence of counseling by clergy and/or a psychologist or psychiatrist. The revised canons specify that if marital unity is imperiled by dissention, it shall be the duty of either or both parties, before contemplating legal action, to lay the matter before a Minister of this Church; and it shall be the duty of such Minister to labor that the parties may be reconciled.

Thus, counseling is required both before the divorce (if the problem ends in divorce) and before the proposed remarriage. It is also required "that continuing concern be shown for the well-being of the former spouse, and of any children of the prior marriage."

The revised canons represent an attempt on the part of the church to uphold both law and grace, judgment and mercy. They do not, as some say, make divorce easier (I have never seen a divorce that has not exacted anguish and pain from those involved), but rather they require that the priest-counselor take an active role in a process which often involves pain as well as hope.

Marriage is not made Christian by bells, bridal marches, and holy words cast upon the proceedings. It is made Christian by the will of the couple, who see it as God's calling to them. The priest never asks of them, "Do you love each other?" but "Will you love each other?" Love, like prayer, is often a matter of the will. "This is my commandment that you love one another as I have loved you" (John 15:19-12, one of the readings at a marriage). Whatever else marriage may signify, to St. Paul it represented "the mystical union that is between Christ and his Church," hence it is a form of Christian discipleship. The priest does not "perform" the marriage, for the couple marry each other in the exchange of vows. The priest only blesses the marriage. The will to love, to bear, believe and hope all things about each other is nourished by prayer, the asking and receiving of forgiveness in good times and in bad. The failure of that will does not nullify God's offering of forgiveness in the failure of the marriage and the possibility of new beginnings.

An ancient tradition of the marriage ceremony is the Eucharist. This represents the first meal of the couple after they are married, one which the congregation should be invited to share, as the community of faith prays together that the couple may walk together with their Lord as his disciples in marriage.

Visitation of the Sick

The author of Hebrews writes, "do not regard lightly the discipline of the Lord, nor lose courage when you are punished by him" (Hebrews

12:5). While the ancient concept of illness as sent by God to test us is a concept that should rightly be rejected in many instances (Jesus consistently ascribed illness to Satan), there is a sense in which it invites a discipline in which the disciple is brought to wholeness. Illness often affords opportunities for reordering our priorities, for reflection, for coming to terms with the need for a disciplined life that has not been ours. On the other hand, illness can cripple and paralyze the will, requiring spiritual strength beyond ourselves.

Suspicion surrounds (and in some cases rightly so) "faith healers" who seem not only to be tasteless and tacky, but seem to use some kind of trickery to "psych" the victim out of his illness. Is it not better, some ask, to face the probable truth rather than the illusion of miracles?

Others view the healings of Jesus as simply the exercise of folk cures in an age which naively assumed the existence of demonic spirits. Still others affirm them as signs given early Christians of the power of God, but now no longer necessary because medical science is available.

In responding to these criticisms of faith healers, it must be acknowledged that healing does come through faith—the faith of the patient either in the doctor or in God, or both, and indeed the faith of others surrounding the patient. Doctors have reported the faith of patients in placebos, which have made them feel better.

As for the responsibility to tell the truth to the patient, it has been my experience and that of others that, from time to time, terminal prognoses are not always realized. Our fates are not necessarily determined by the diagnosis. I have seen people to whom no hope has been given refuse to accept the diagnosis, leave the hospital and experience apparent healing.

This is not to deprecate medical science, for it is part of the dominion God shares with us. In the thirty-eighth chapter of Ecclesiasticus we are told that the doctor "too has been created by the Lord . . . the Lord has brought medicines into existence from the earth, and the sensible man will not despise them." Certainly the cause of healing is ill served by triumphant and exclusive claims, on the part of those in medicine or in spiritual healing, that their means and methodology are alone responsible for the healing of a patient.

It is evident that Jesus appointed the twelve not only to preach but to "have authority to cast out demons" (Mark 3:15). This commission is given to the church. The word *holy* literally means "wholeness." *Salvation* is another word for wholeness. Indeed the word *religion* is derived from a Latin word which means "to bind together."

Soul and body—the spirit, our psyche, our physical being—are a unity. Ancient man knew what modern psychiatry is discovering, namely that guilt, anxiety, and unresolved inner conflict create physical symptoms. I read about a doctor at the Mayo Clinic who believed that at least sixty percent of the patients he saw were possessed by problems spiritual in nature.

As we noted, Holy Communion may be given at the Visitation to the Sick. The presence of my communion set occasionally raises an apprehensive glance from the patient, with the unspoken question, "Is all going well? If so why are you here with the last rites?" My receiving communion with a patient states that I am less than whole. I need healing and forgiveness.

We have noted the importance of forgiveness, which is part of the discipline asked of the sick. The General Confession we pray together on Sundays and other times presents the truth that sin is corporate, we are members of one another and sinners to each other.[2]

The discipline of confession to a priest is often essential to the healing process, following as it does upon a period of counseling. One of the forms this kind of confession can take is called "Healing of Memories," a service I perform frequently. Here we confess the traumas and experiences of being hurt, the presence of guilt and unconfessed anxieties. God is not limited to our present, but can be invoked through the Holy Spirit to heal our past, which has determined us in negative ways. After all, the word *sin* does not only mean a specific act; it comes from a word which means "to miss the mark." Confession and absolution, followed by repentance—the desire to do an about-face, to make restitution and initiate reconciliation—are necessary to spiritual healing. Spiritual healing may manifest itself in the healing of bodily diseases.

Another means of healing, noted in Mark 6:13, is unction or anointing with oil. Traditionally, the oil is blessed by the bishop in his cathedral on Maundy Thursday. We are familiar with "extreme unction" associated with "the last rites"; but originally oil was an outward and visible sacrament of healing and today is experiencing renewed usage for that purpose. The oil symbolizes the apostolic presence of the bishop. In ancient times olive oil was a standard staple for medicinal purposes, but to us it represents a visible means of continuity with the early church. In the Epistle of James (5:14) we see the church as the first hospital, with the elders of the church being summoned to anoint the sick. "Thou anointest my head with oil" (Psalm 23) affirms oil as the sign of peace, wholeness, and well being.

Just as prayer cannot be reduced to one technique, so also prayer for healing, unction, the touch of the human hand are ways healing is expressed. Jesus healed in a variety of ways: He used the faith of others; he called upon the faith of the sick person; he used dust and spittle; he issued commands. Jesus did not assume that all illness was the express will of God. In the thirteenth chapter of St. Matthew in the parable of the wheat and tares, we note that it was the "enemy"—the principalities and powers of darkness—which invaded God's good creation.

While illness, as noted, may signal opportunities for needed reflection on our life, it can also plunge us into a depression that often renders us incapable of believing any healing or hope is possible. The tragic truth about much "faith healing" is that it puts the patient in the position of trying to manifest faith which he or she does not feel. To have faith becomes a burden.

But, in the story of the widow's mite and the parable of the mustard seed, we note that God can work with very little. Our Lord was once confronted by an anguished man who wanted his daughter to be healed. "I believe," he said, "help thou my unbelief" (Mark 9:24). Our Lord accepted him, as he accepts us, even with our doubt.

The faith of others is available to us so that our faith may be nourished. Too often we clergy discover that we were not called, thus becoming helpless hearers after the fact.

It has been said that "all of us are terminal cases." While spiritual healing may lead to the lengthening of our life, its real purpose is to bring us to wholeness, to the renewal of our faith. A patient may receive competent surgery and be given miracle drugs, but if the inner man is depressed, possessed of unresolved conflict and guilt, a prolonged life has no meaning. Who among us has not known of someone who in fact has decided not to get well and has succeeded in remaining ill? Who among us has not known of someone who has used illness as a means of manipulating others? Thus Jesus asked the cripple at the pool of Siloam who had been going there for so long, "Do you want to be healed?"

Our complete healing is experienced only when we pass through the doors of death. But we can die filled with resentment and fear, the absence of all hope, or we can die well. In spiritual healing we have a foretaste of the life to come, intimations of what perfect wholeness will be, beyond this life.

Death

The first service I attended in an Episcopal church was a funeral. Because the occasion involved the premature death of the daughter of a prominent member of that congregation, I anticipated banks of flowers, certainly a eulogy. I was deeply moved by the simplicity of the service. The congregation sang hymns of resurrection, as though it were Easter. The Scriptures were read, psalms were said, and the congregation recited the Apostles' Creed, which was followed by prayers not only commending the departed life to her Lord and maker, but speaking to us the living as well.

Just as sex was unmentionable in the Victorian era, so in our time death has become the final embarrassment—the unmentionable. It is difficult to say someone has "died." "Passed away" comes easier. The denial of death is dramatized by hermetically sealed coffins encased in heavy steel vaults; and around the grave the earth is masked in fake grass.

I do not believe it is totally fair to blame funeral directors for what has come to be known as "the American way of death." I have found most funeral directors to be sensitive and willing to go out of their way to help. But they cannot be faulted for giving us what we think we want. Guilt often accompanies a death and, out of guilt, we give to the departed by compensating for what we did not give in life.

Death brings with it an appropriate discipline in the traditions of our church. First, the clergy are to be notified by the family so prayers can be offered with the family. The church, not the funeral home, is the place for Christian burial service. As with weddings, the only flowers permitted are on the altar. Hymns reflecting resurrection faith are appropriate.

The coffin should be as inexpensive as possible. Responding to this trend, the St. Francis Burial Society in Washington offers simple wooden coffins for a few hundred dollars. They can be ordered in kit form. As it comes into the church the coffin is covered with a pall—white or purple with Christian symbolism. The coffin is not seen.

Unless the cemetery requires it, the use of a vault is unnecessary. Being buried in a wooden coffin without a vault permits us to return quickly to the earth from which we came. The ritual casting of earth upon the coffin during the commital dramatizes this truth.

Increasingly, many are willing their bodies to medical schools. In this case the funeral can be held without the body and, at a later time, the commital service for the body can be held. Cremation is appropriate and some of our churches are providing crypts for the ashes on the church grounds or places for their scattering.

Thus the discipline which surrounds the event of death is not a discipline to be altered to reflect the personalities of those involved. The discipline is the same for all of us, including the clergy.

The Eucharist, an ancient part of the ritual surrounding death, is most appropriate at this time as it proclaims in the post communion prayer, "Grant that this Sacrament may be unto us a comfort in affliction, and a pledge of our inheritance in that kingdom where there is no death . . ." (Prayer Book, p. 482).

Nowhere is what we believe about death said better than in the service of Christian Burial. Perhaps more so than any other service, this one has been a means of bringing many into the fellowship of our church through its simple dignity and merciful brevity.

X. Life after Death

Death, as described by Shakespeare's Hamlet, is "that undiscovered country from whose bourne no traveller returns." We regard it with fear and fascination. We fear it because we do not know what it ultimately means for us. Indeed we resent it because it represents a final judgment upon our scientific techniques to sustain life. It is an embarrassment.

We are fascinated by death for the same reasons that we fear it. We are fascinated by the unknown. Our fascination has been fed by reports of those who have clinically died and had out-of-the-body experiences—some blissful, confirming some traditional imagery, and some painful, seemingly confirming the presence of a hell.

There have always been those who take comfort in the prospect of personal extinction, drifting out, as they believe, into nothingness as smoke into the night. The ancient Hebrew, however, regarded such a prospect with terror for he feared the loss of the identity which came from having a body.

As we know, all cultures project their visions of the afterlife—happy hunting grounds, streets of gold, compensation for what was not had here. For those who have valued the creative opportunities of their life, heaven will offer an extension of creativity. For those who have dedicated themselves to the task of being self-righteous, heaven will afford a view of those receiving their just payment for not being righteous. In his biting satire, *Letters from the Earth*, Mark Twain suggests that it is extraordinary that heaven represents for many pious Christians the absence of those things they coveted on earth, yet pretend not to value in their future existence.

Traditionally, heaven's rewards were meant to motivate good behavior and morality. "Good" people go to heaven. However, our advanced culture has given us such good things in our here-and-now that it is hard to imagine heaven providing more conveniences. As for the graphic horrors of hell, presented to inspire right belief and behavior, what can Dante offer in his *Inferno* that can compare with the concentration camps?

There are many who believe neither in heaven nor hell but who seem happy and exhibit compassion, sensitivity, goodness and morality. I think we must take seriously some of the criticisms they have advanced against the ways some Christians use the concept of heaven and hell.

I will mention only one of them, but one which commands a wide audience. It is derived in large measure from the writings of Sigmund Freud and his followers. In essence, he suggested that doctrines of the afterlife, even belief in God, are projections of our inner needs and anxieties. Thus the future life is a projection to satisfy a neurosis.

But both the believer and the agnostic are still confronted with the mystery of the question of ancient Job, "If a man die shall he live again?" How is it that man knows that he will die? How does he know the name for death? Where do our fantasies (if they are that) about the afterlife come from? Why do we even raise the question about personal survival unless, as St. Augustine put it, "Thou has made us for thyself, O Lord, and our hearts find no rest until they rest in thee." Were there no water how could we thirst? If death ends all, how could we raise the question about other possibilities?

While this is no proof to the atheist or agnostic, a conviction still persists, a suspicion on the part of many of us that our hopes and longings are ultimately to be answered.

The Bible

Although Scripture states clearly that there is an afterlife, there is no clear and consistent picture presented, rather a variety of perspectives. In the story our Lord told about Dives and Lazarus (Luke 16), when Dives wanted to send word back to his brothers of his experience in hell, Abraham, his custodian, offered the interesting observation that if Dives' brothers did not believe in God and the existence of an afterlife, not even the appearance of one from the dead would convince them. This is why our Lord occasionally refused to use signs to confirm his power when he was asked to do so. Signs have authenticity only to those who wish to believe. Signs may confirm faith; they do not create it.

On the basis of this story, many have believed that the fiery torments here refer to the state of the damned. It must be noted, however, that in the New Testament two words—Gehenna and Hades—are both translated as *hell. Hades,* the Greek version of the Hebrew *sheol,* was not a place of fiery torment but the abode of all of the dead until resurrection, where the dead lived as "shades," a kind of half-life.

Gehenna had its origin under the evil Hebrew king Manassas, who practiced infant sacrifice in the valley of Hinnom. In time this valley on the outskirts of Jerusalem became a perpetually burning refuse heap, symbolizing desolation and horror. More than one rabbi used it to make a point.

The afterlife is a spiritual existence, one in which happiness and pain are involved. In fielding a difficult question put to him by some Pharisees regarding whose wife a woman would be in the afterlife, Jesus concluded that "in the resurrection they neither marry nor are given in marriage, but are like angels in heaven" (Matthew 22:30). Any significant experience is one of the spirit, be it one of joy and fulfillment or one of despair and suffering. Marlowe's Mephistopheles said to Dr. Faustus, "I Myself am Hell." Heaven and hell are part of our existence.

The Bible has been used both to support and refute speculation as to whether or not we have a second chance. Both of these convictions are grounded in what God's justice and righteousness seem to require. For example, in Hebrews 6:4 it is said, ". . . it is impossible to restore again to repentance those who have once been enlightened". But does this refer to the afterlife or life now?

In support of the belief that hell is not eternal or the punishment of those in hell not eternal is the observation that the Greek word for eternal may be translated age, or a period of time, or an eon. St. Paul affirmed in I Corinthians 15:28 that "God shall be all in all."

Using the Bible this way is ultimately futile because we tend to ascribe to divine intent our prejudices and presuppositions. In Jesus Christ God is present in both love and judgment. The ministry of Jesus Christ reveals a God who loves us so much that he will permit us not to love him, which is another way of permitting us the experience of hell. We are, in a real sense, architects of the heaven and hell in which we live.

It appears to me that we might imagine our life, if drawn on a graph, moving in one of two directions—either away from self and toward God or moving deeply into self and ego. But by self, I mean not a healthy and basic need for self-knowledge or the proper love of one's self commanded by our Lord, but an obsession with what I call the unholy Trinity of I, Me, and Myself. Neither of these lines on our graph will be a straight one. It will rise and fall, indicating peak experiences, periods of selflessness and surrender to and adoration of God, the giving and receiving of love, as well as valleys of despair, irresponsibility, and egocentricity.

Beyond this life, we continue to live, moving either more and more into the presence of God or toward the hell of absolute self with all that this implies. There is a story attributed to an old monk where hell is described as a large room with an open door; one is free to leave at any time, but those there cannot imagine anything better than what they have! The hell of hell is that it is without hope, the imagination is dead.

If we choose to live our life without prayer, adoration and worship, forgiveness sought and given, why do we suppose that we will necessarily turn to God in a future life? But those who have hungered and thirsted for God in this life will continue to love him and want to know him more deeply, opening to him as flowers open to the sun in the light of the life beyond.

The Burial Office begins with our Lord's proclamation, "I am the resurrection and the life," and then continues with the affirmation of Job, "I know that my redeemer liveth . . . and though this body be destroyed, yet shall I see God; whom I shall see for myself. . . ." Specifics are shrouded in mystery.

C. S. Lewis observed that, if we lived in "flatland," a two dimensional world, how could we understand the report of a third dimension or for that matter a fourth or fifth one? Heaven and hell can only be described in symbolic language, because we are dealing with a state of being, not a place. The Scripture affirms, however, that we will not be disembodied spirits but will have a spiritual body appropriate to our life there (I Corinthians 15).

The Teaching of the Church

Protestants have traditionally believed that, following death, there is immediate removal either to heaven or hell. This was largely in reaction to the exploitative and legalistic doctrine of purgatory, so much a part of the piety of the medieval world. The doctrine of purgatory attests to what has always been a strong, intuitive feeling in religious man, that a process of purgation and preparation is needed before one can experience God fully. This is represented in the Collect for Purity at the Eucharist: "cleanse the thoughts of our hearts. . . ."

There are Scriptural passages which tend to support this doctrine. The parable of the unforgiving servant (Matthew 18:21) states that this man can not be released from prison until he pays his just debts (he had refused to release others from their debts). In Psalm 66 there is the sentence, "We went through fire and water, yet thou has brought us forth into a spacious place." Both of these passages may well relate to life here and now.

Atonement or sacrifice for the dead, who are considered to be in a state of sin, is mentioned in the Apocrypha in the Book of II Maccabees 12:43–45. As noted, for purposes of faith and doctrine, Protestants and Anglicans do not hold the Apocrypha on the same level as the Scriptures they deem to be canonical.

These Scriptures and others illustrate the origin of this belief, and it must be remembered that the primary reason the doctine of purgatory was rejected by Protestant reformers was because of its use in the selling of indulgences.

Whereas in the twenty-second Article of Religion the Church of England officially rejected "the Romish doctrine of Purgatory," the Anglican Church did not reject the belief that the souls of the departed are to be prayed for, that we are in pilgrimage following death. The Prayer Book (except in its 1552 edition) has consistently provided prayers commemorating the dead. At the Burial Office we pray that, "increasing in knowledge and love of thee *he* may go from strength to strength in the life of perfect service in thy heavenly kingdom. . . ." We pray for the dead as we pray for those we love who are absent from us. We pray not by trying to influence God's attitude toward them, but by affirming our common pilgrimage and mortality.

That state of future life is paradise. It has for many the same meaning as heaven, although a distinction between the two should be made. Paradise literally means "the garden." Old Testament usage of this word reflects various meanings. Sometimes it describes the restoration of nature upon the earth; sometimes it refers to a future state; but it always carries the connotation of refreshment and rest.

Our Lord upon the cross said to the thief being crucified with him, "Today thou wilt be with me in paradise." The church fathers called the intermediate state paradise. Again, Scripture provides us with little detail. Although we often use the word *sleep* to describe this condition in paradise, we note in Revelation 6:9–11 the implication that we are conscious, as is also implied in Hebrews 12:1: "Therefore since we are surrounded by so great a cloud of witnesses. . . ."

Heaven, traditionally, is that state of being following paradise. At the time of the "general resurrection," according to one ancient theory, we will be given bodies. We will be complete and thus experience the beatific vision of God, seeing him as he is, in heaven.

While there are variations upon these views which have been the subject of much speculation, the affirmation that "Now I know in part; then I shall understand fully" (I Corinthians 13:12) does persist. There also persists the affirmation that, as our heavenly Father notes the fall of the sparrow and the numbering of the hairs upon our head (Matthew 10:29), so are we known of God in our individuality, our uniqueness. We do not know the form of the resurrection body which will manifest recognition, but we believe, as St. Paul put it, that we shall be "clothed." Who we are as persons will persist.

Spiritualism

There are many words which have a positive meaning, but develop a negative meaning when an *ism* is attached. *Spiritualism* is one such word. It has come to mean ways of seeking contact and communion with the dead. From the dawn of religious consciousness, the possibility of communication with the dead has been a subject of fascination.

Are we to be bound by such biblical taboos as, for example, Saul seeking guidance from the Witch of Endor? Are we bound by other injunctions from the Old Testament forbidding traffic with wizards and seers, skilled in the arts of necromancy (Deuteronomy 18:11)? Some Christians would say that we are not, because these ancient taboos have been neutralized by Christ. Why, they would reason, should we not seek communication with our loved ones? Indeed, there are those who claim consolation from alleged messages from the dead.

It is impossible to refute an experience which has brought apparent consolation. However, I do believe that the traditional teaching of the church, which has been against this practice, is not without wisdom. In counseling those who have been involved in attempts to communicate with the dead, I have noticed that these alleged contacts, far from bringing peace or a measure of assurance, create states of anxiety and depression. Moreover, they often signify a desperate desire to confirm faith.

Secularism creates the need to explore the transcendent, the otherworldly. Movies and books such as *The Exorcist* represent a deep hunger on the part of many to experience something of the beyond. It is almost as though, if we can still believe in demonic possession, we can still believe in God. Astrology, the occult, and drugs are ways of getting in touch with nonrational realities, drugs being a means of synthetic salvation. When St. Paul spoke about "principalities and powers," the "elemental spirits of the universe," he was affirming that there are dark powers over against God which can seduce and destroy us. As Christians, we are not predestined by the stars but by loyalty to our Lord. Occult practices tend to create a fascination and hunger which feeds upon itself.

While I have experienced revelations in dreams, and while I appreciate accounts of psychic experience, I believe that those who seek the seance and the "control" are manipulated and manipulative. The church has taught us that God gives us what we need. The gifts of the Spirit are the gifts of a God who may give us dreams, prophecies, and revelation in which we are granted visions of the beyond. To be open and receptive is one thing; to employ techniques to seek out revelation is another.

The focal point of our communion with the departed is the altar. When we affirm our belief in the "communion of saints," we give thanks "with angels and archangels and with all the company of heaven. . . ." The altar is not a seance table, but that place which dramatizes our everlasting communion with those whom we love but no longer see. Such Scriptures of assurance as Romans 8:38, which affirms that nothing "in all creation will be able to separate us from the love of God in Christ Jesus our Lord," are crucial to our faith. As I noted earlier, "If they do not hear Moses and the prophets neither will they be convinced if some one should rise from the dead" (Luke 16:31).

The Second Coming

The creeds affirm "He shall come again with glory to judge the living and the dead." I once heard the cynical quip that, since most of us missed the meaning of his first coming, why should we think our perception will be improved by the second one. However, his coming again "with glory" implies that his appearance will be beyond doubt.

Today we are inundated by books and teachings on the Second Coming. The books of Hal Lindsey have been most popular, especially *The Late, Great Planet Earth.* [3] Biblical prophecies are applied to our times, suggesting that the ingredients of the last days are present or are in the process of fulfillment. Lindsey cites the rebirth of the Jewish nation of Israel and its possession of Jerusalem as an indication of partial fulfillment of the prophecy. Although the Temple has not yet been rebuilt upon the historic site of Mt. Moriah (because there is a Moslem holy place there), it is in the offing.

Passages from the Book of Revelation can be considered fulfilled in the rise of communism, particularly in China. The future Fuehrer will rule from Rome, having come back from the dead. The ecumenical movement will become a force in service to antichrist. The presence of widespread drug addiction is further evidence of the decline of the West. And so it goes. Yet, after all of this, a righteous remnant will remain to carry on the true worship of God and the true believers will be rescued from the world as it plunges into destruction.

The "rapture," described by St. Paul in I Thessalonians 4:16 has to do with the descent of Christ from heaven and the sweeping into the clouds of the righteous to join him. Some believe that this will occur before the Great Tribulation (the rule of antichrist upon earth), some believe it will occur during the Tribulation, and others believe it will happen after the Tribulation. There are those who believe in millenarianism, an ancient belief (held by Adventists) which presumes a thousand year period of blessedness upon earth, followed by the Second Coming.

Apocalypticism is an ancient theme in Jewish and Christian thought. All apocalypticism looks forward to a dramatic confrontation between God and his legions and the forces of the antichrist. While some Jewish writers believed that this kingdom would be fulfilled within history and expected a restoration of nature with peace and harmony among man and beast under the reign of an earthly messiah, others saw it as an order that would be imposed from without. With the experience of tribulation and persecution, many looked for recompense and vindication from beyond. This is a theme of apocalyptic literature.

At the outset of the persecutions, the early Christians saw the Roman emperor as the personification of the antichrist. The Book of Revelation, with its mysterious imagery, reflected the hope of the reward of the faithful—a glorious counterpart to the tribulations being experienced by the saints on earth.

When the emphasis on futurism began to wane, the church began to order itself, creating disciplines for discipleship. In time, the imagery of apocalyptic prophecies was applied to the Catholic Church by those suffering persecution as heretics. The pope became the antichrist. In later times the antichrist was identified with tyrannical rulers—Napoleon, Mussolini, Hitler, Stalin, and Mao. No religious denomination has a corner on apocalypticism. Whenever the social order is deeply troubled, whenever there is war, famine, the collapse of law and order, apocalypticism thrives.

Some time ago, there appeared the following paragraph, a seeming comment on our times, on the front page of a newspaper:

It is a gloomy moment in the history of our country. Not in the lifetime of most men has there been so much grave and deep apprehension: never has the future seemed so incalculable as at this time. The domestic economic situation is in chaos. Our dollar is weak throughout the world. Prices are so high as to be utterly impossible. The political cauldron seethes and bubbles with uncertainty. Russia hangs, as usual, like a cloud, dark and silent upon the horizon. It is a solemn moment. Of our troubles, no man can see the end *(Harpers' Weekly,* October 1857).

As the author of Ecclesiastes put it, "There is nothing new under the sun." What *is* new is that our technology has created a way to bring about an instant Armageddon. The apocalypse can be of our own making, either by violent destruction or by the slower process of pollution.

But we are not determined by prophecy. To view the Bible as a kind of codebook featuring a timetable for the earth's destruction is to burden it with a false reading and interpretation. A prophet is primarily a "forthteller," not a foreteller. The prophets of Israel in their time, as well as Jesus in his time, told forth what God was doing. If their messages often involved predictions of violence and destruction, they were always accompanied by the conviction that this is God's world, and he wills its wholeness.

As far as I am concerned, the subject of the end of the world is academic, irresolvable, and irrelevant. Our Lord said, "But of that day or that hour no one knows, not even the angels in heaven, not the Son, but only the Father" (Mark 13:32). The end of the world, for us, comes with our death. The end of the world also comes at times in our life when we experience defeat, death, despair, rejection, and meaninglessness. On the other hand, our world comes alive for us when we come to experience wholeness, the knowledge that we are loved, when we can affirm promise and hope. There is a lapel button which asks, "Is there life after birth?" This is the real question to which the gospel gives affirmation.

"It is an unfaithful generation that seeks after a sign," said our Lord. The sign given to all of us is the sign of the cross. It is made over the font of baptism and over the earth at our burial. Its meaning is always beyond our complete understanding, but we trust in it in life and we trust in it in death. Even those who deny it must in some way come to terms with it.

Each time the cross goes before the procession of choir and clergy and passes by us the people of God bow at its passing, for it leads us to the place of Calvary and to the glory of resurrection. It leads us to the One who comes forth to meet us in word and in sacrament.

Somewhere I once read, "I do not know what the future holds, but I do know who holds the future."

Chapter Notes

Chapter I
Jesus or Christianity?

1. Kirby Page, *Jesus or Christianity* (New York: Doubleday, 1929).

2. Rosemary Haughton, *Why Be a Christian?* (Philadelphia: J. B. Lippincott Co., 1968), p. 14.

3. Malcolm Muggeridge, *Jesus Rediscovered* (New York: Doubleday, 1979).

4. Albert Schweitzer, *The Quest of the Historical Jesus* (New York: Macmillan Co., 1957), p. 403.

Chapter II
The Church as an Institution

1. Massey Shepherd, *The Paschal Liturgy and the Apocalypse* (Richmond, Va.: John Knox Press, 1960).

2. Massey Shepherd, *The Worship of the Church* (New York: The Seabury Press, 1952), p. 4.

3. Urban T. Holmes, III, *To Speak of God* (New York: The Seabury Press, 1974), p. 41.

4. Claude B. Moss, *The Christian Faith* (London: S.P.C.P., 1977), p. 387.

Chapter III
Church History

1. Powell Mills Dawley, *Chapters in Church History* (New York: The Seabury Press, 1950), p. 16.

2. Ibid., p. 16.

Chapter IV
The Early British Church

1. Powell Mills Dawley, *Chapters in Church History, rev. ed.* (New York: The Seabury Press, 1966), p. 118.

Chapter V
The Bible

1. F. G. Kenyon, *The Story of the Bible* (London: J. Murray, 1936), pp. 33f.

2. William Barclay, *Introducing the Bible* (Nashville: Abingdon Press, 1972), p. 139.

Chapter VIII
Prayer and the Prayer Book

1. Depression is not necessarily a condition that should be medicated away, but it may hold clues to our healing. It may be of God. Paradoxically, our inner darkness may provide light (see Isaiah 45:7).

2. See, especially, William B. Williamson, *A Handbook for Episcopalians,* rev. ed. (Wilton, CT: Morehouse Publishing, 1979).

Chapter IX
The Church's Discipline

1. Jacques Ellul, *Prayer and Modern Man* (New York: The Seabury Press, 1970), p. 16.

2. An excellent recent treatment of this theme is found in Carl Menninger's book, *Whatever Became of Sin?* (New York: Hawthorn Books, 1970).

3. Hal Lindsey, *The Late Great Planet Earth* (Grand Rapids, Mich.: Zondervan, 1970).

Bibliography

Bible

Anderson, Bernhard W., *Understanding the Old Testament.* Englewood Cliffs, N.J.: Prentice Hall, 2nd ed., 1966.

Barclay, William, *Introducing the Bible.* Nashville: Abingdon Press, 1972.

Bruce, F. F., *New Testament History.* New York: Doubleday & Co., Anchor Book ed., 1972.

Cassels, Louis, *Your Bible.* New York: Funk & Wagnalls, 1967.

Dentan, Robert C., *The Holy Scriptures: A Survey.* New York: The Seabury Press, 1961.

Fuller, Reginald, and Wright, G. Ernest, *The Book of the Acts of God.* New York: Doubleday & Co., 1957.

Gottwald, Norman K., *A Light to the Nations.* New York: Harper & Row, 1959.

Napier, B. Davie, *From Faith to Faith.* New York: Harper & Brothers, 1955.

Price, James L., *Interpreting the New Testament.* New York: Holt, Rinehard & Winston, 1961.

Wenham, John W., *Christ and the Bible.* Downers Grove, Ill.: Inter-Varsity Press, 1973.

Stott, John R. W., *Understanding the Bible.* Glendale, Calif.: Regal Books Division, G/L Publications, 1973.

Church History

Addison, J. T., *The Episcopal Church in the United States 1789-1931.* Hamden, CT: The Shoe String Press, Inc., 1969.

Bainton, Roland H., *The Reformation of the Sixteenth Century.* Boston: The Beacon Press, 1952.

Bettenson, Henry, *Documents of the Christian Church.* New York: Oxford University Press, 1947.

Chadwick, Owen, *The Mind of the Oxford Movement.* Stanford, Calif.: Stanford University Press, 1960.

Dawley, Powell Mills, *Chapters in Church History.* New York: The Seabury Press, 1966.

——————————, *Our Christian Heritage.* Wilton, CT: Morehouse Publishing, 1978.

Deanesley, Margaret, *The Pre-Conquest Church in England.* New York: Oxford University Press, 1961.

Dillenberger, John W., and Welch, Claude, *Protestant Christianity.* New York: Charles Scribner's Sons, 1954.

Enslin, Morton Scott, *Christian Beginnings.* New York: Harper & Brothers, 1956.

Moorman, J. R. H., *A History of the Church in England.* Wilton, CT: Morehouse Publishing, 1967.

Neill, Stephen, *Anglicanism.* New York: Oxford University Press, 1977.

Nichols, James Hastings, *History of Christianity 1650–1950.* New York: Ronald Press, 1956.

Sweet, William Warren, *The Story of Religion in America.* New York: Harper & Brothers, 1950.

Walker, Williston, *A History of the Christian Church.* New York: Charles Scribner's Sons, 1959.

Doctrine in the Church of England and the Episcopal Church

Bernardin, J. B., *An Introduction to the Episcopal Church.* Wilton, CT: Morehouse Publishing, 1978.

Kirk K. E. (ed.), *The Apostolic Ministry.* London: Hodder & Stoughton, 1957.

Paton, David M. (ed.), *Essays in Anglican Self Criticism.* London: SCM Press, 1958.

Pike, James A., and Pittenger, W. Norman, *The Faith of the Church.* New York: The Seabury Press, 1951.

Ramsey, Arthur Michael, *Introducing the Christian Faith.* Wilton, CT: Morehouse Publishing, 1961.

Selwyn, Edward Gordon (ed.), *Essays Catholic & Critical.* London: S.P.C.K., 1958.

Wilson, Frank E., *Faith and Practice.* Wilton, CT: Morehouse Publishing, 1941.

Liturgy and Worship

Allison, C. Fitzsimons, *Fear, Love, and Worship*. Wilton, CT: Morehouse Publishing, 1988.

Babin, David E., *Introduction to the Liturgy of the Lord's Supper*. Wilton, CT: Morehouse Publishing, 1968.

_____, *The Celebration of Life: Our Changing Liturgy*. Wilton, CT: Morehouse Publishing, 1969.

Hatchett, Marion, *Sanctifying Life, Time and Space: An Introduction to Liturgical Study*. New York: The Seabury Press, 1976.

Shepherd, Massey H., Jr., *The Reform of Liturgical Worship*. New York: Oxford University Press, 1961.

Theology (General)

Cassels, Louis, *A Christian Primer*. New York: Doubleday & Co., 1967.

Dentan, Robert C., *A First Reader in Biblical Theology*. New York: The Seabury Press, 1961.

Holmes, Urban T., III, *To Speak of God*. New York: The Seabury Press, 1974.

Macquarrie, John, *Principles of Christian Theology*. New York: Charles Scribner's Sons, 1966.

Peerman, Dean G., and Marty, Martin E. (ed.), *A Handbook of Christian Theologians*. Cleveland: The World Publishing Co., 1965.

Schaeffer, Francis, *He is There and He is Not Silent*. Wheaton, Ill.: Tyndale House Publishers, 1972.

_____, *Escape from Reason*. Downers Grove, Ill.: Inter-Varsity Press, 1968.

_____, *The God Who is There*. Downers Grove, Ill.: Inter-Varsity Press, 1968.

Sykes, Stephen, *An Introduction to Christian Theology Today*. Atlanta: John Knox Press, American Edition, 1971.

Tillich, Paul, *A Complete History of Christian Thought*. New York: Harper & Brothers, 1968.

Whale, J. S., *Christian Doctrine*. Cambridge: The University Press, 1952.

The Spiritual Life

Bloom, Anthony, *Beginning to Pray*. New York: Paulist Press, 1970.

Bonhoeffer, Dietrich, *The Cost of Discipleship*. New York: The Macmillan Co., 1967.

Buber, Martin, *I and Thou*. New York: Charles Scribner's Sons, 1957.

Buttrick, George A., *Prayer*. New York: Abingdon Cokesbury Press, 1942.

Ellul, Jacques, *Prayer and Modern Man*. New York: The Seabury Press, 1970.

Gibbard, Mark, *Why Pray?* Valley Forge, PA: The Judson Press, 1971.

Kelly, Thomas R., *A Testament of Devotion*. New York: Harper & Brothers, 1941.

Kempis, Thomas à, *The Imitation of Christ*. New Canaan, CT: Keats Publishing Co., 1973.

MacNutt, Francis, *Healing*. New York: Bantam Books, 1977.

Macquarrie, John, *Paths in Spirituality*. New York: Harper & Row, 1972.

Miller, Keith, *The Taste of New Wine*. Waco, TX: Word Books, 1973.

Nee, Watchman, *A Table in the Wilderness*. Fort Washington, Pa.: Christian Literature Crusade, 1973.

Nouwen, Henri J. M., *The Genesee Diary: Report from a Trappist Monastery*. New York: Doubleday & Co. Inc., 1976.

—————————, *Reaching Out: The Three Movements of Spiritual Life*. New York: Doubleday & Co., 1975.

Packer, J. I., *Knowing God*. Downers Grove, Ill.: Inter-Varsity Press, 1973.

Quoist, Michael, *Prayers of Life*. Dublin, NH: Gill & Macmillan, 1969.

Russell, A. J. (ed.), *God Calling*. Old Tappan, N.J.: Fleming H. Revell, 1979.

Sanford, Agnes, *The Healing Light*. St. Paul, Minn.: Macalester Park Co., 1968.

Terwilliger, Robert E., *Christian Believing*. Wilton, CT: Morehouse Publishing, 1973.

Jesus Christ

Ainger, Geoffrey, *Jesus Our Contemporary*. New York: The Seabury Press, 1967.

Barrett, C. K., *Jesus and the Gospel Tradition*. Philadelphia: The Fortress Press, 1968.

Bornkamm, Gunther, *Jesus of Nazareth*. New York: Harper & Brothers, 1960.

Chesterton, G. K., *The Everlasting Man*. Garden City, N.Y.: Image Books, Doubleday & Co., Inc., 1955.

Muggeridge, Malcolm, *Jesus Rediscovered*. Wheaton, Ill.: Tyndale House, 1972.